Restoring the

Village, Values,

and Commitment

Solutions for the Black Family

Jawanza
Kunjufu

Revised edition, first printing 2002
Front cover design by Angelo Williams

Printed in the United States of America

ISBN: 0-913543-80-2

African American Images
Chicago, Illinois

Table of Contents

Introduction..iv

Chapter One
    The Power, Passion, and Pain of Black Love............1

Chapter Two
    The First Generation 21

Chapter Three
    Love, Commitment, and Marriage........................37

Chapter Four
    Fatherhood..61

Chapter Five
    Motherhood...83

Chapter Six
    Childhood..103

Chapter Seven
    Values: The Keys to the Family............................115

Chapter Eight
    The Nigger Spirit..129

Chapter Nine
    Insult Level..137

Chapter Ten
    Restoring the Village...143

Chapter Eleven
    Cultural Myths...163

Notes...184

Introduction

*But if anyone does not provide for his own
and especially for those of his household,
he has denied the faith and is worse
than an unbeliever.
1 Timothy 5:8. New King James Version*

I thank the Lord for the opportunity to write this book on the Black Family. Each year the Lord has been gracious enough to give me the knowledge to write a book. I have no idea before the year begins, what will be the subject. I try patiently to wait for the Lord to give me some sign and this was this year's revelation.

I believe the family is the basic unit of the nation. If you want to find out what the nation is doing, look inside the family. I also believe that Satan is real and hates family. He will do anything and work through anyone who allows him, to destroy the family.

Of all the problems you will read about throughout this book, I believe the most startling is that 66 percent of our children live in single parent homes. Where will the figure stop? It is projected by the year 2010 it will be 70 percent. Will there come a point where no African American children will live with their fathers?

I believe the two greatest factors affecting the African American family are - not being in relationship with God and unemployment. The good news is that both can be solved, in spite of White supremacy. Many of us have become incapacitated by racism. Real power does not come from racists, it comes from God. Scripture says: *Greater is He that is in me, than he that is in the world.*

Our second greatest problem is unemployment. Europeans brought us to this country to work and that reason no longer exists. White America has a problem, what do they do with a people they no longer need? Our question is what are we going to do for ourselves? How can we maximize and leverage our 600 billion dollars? Many of us are not aware that for every billion dollars we spend with foreign businesses we export 30,000 jobs.

Unfortunately, if we admit White supremacy as being our greatest problem and feel impotent in resisting, then as Nathan and Julia Hare point out, when people feel powerless, they turn to "feel good" and self-help activities rather than marshalling their resources to resist oppression.[1]

This book consists of 11 chapters, but before we take a scholarly and quantitative look at the African American family, let's read the first chapter, which is more personal. Maybe you can find yourself in one of these vignettes. It is my prayer that through the remaining chapters, we can use the village to do more than raise a child, but keep the Black family together.

We must feed our relationships, in order for them to grow.

CHAPTER ONE

THE POWER, PASSION, AND PAIN OF BLACK LOVE

The Blood Test

enee and Joseph had been involved with one another for the past 18 months. Joseph at 25 and Renee at 24 had grown to like one another. Joseph worked at UPS and Renee worked as a clerk in one of the local stores. They had became sexually active with each other after the third "encounter." She preferred the term "encounters" when describing their relationship, because Joseph seldom took Renee out on dates. For Renee, a date was when you dressed up, put on heels and went to dinner or a play. Joseph preferred "kicking" it around the house, putting on CD's or watching videos.

While Renee wanted Joseph to talk more and to take her out, both were sexually satisfied. Sometimes Renee would get on Joseph's case about falling asleep before taking care of her "needs," leaving her to "finish" solo in the bathroom. Other than this, everything was fine. Their form of birth control was a combination of the rhythm method, a condom whenever Joseph could find them and the diaphragm when Renee felt like it. She had stopped using the pill after six months because she said it was giving her headaches and making her gain weight.

Joseph used to tease her by saying, "Maybe it's not the pill making you gain weight, but all that ice cream you're eating at night." Renee countered with "You don't seem to have any complaints with these ice cream thighs and behind in the bedroom so you just shut up!"

A few weeks later, Renee told Joseph she was pregnant. Joseph: Baby, what **you** gonna do about it? Renee: What do you mean what am I going to do about it? This is our baby. Joseph: Renee you know what I mean, the baby is in your stomach and I just figured you'd already begun to think about your next step. When are you going to get an abortion? Renee: Why would you think that I would want to abort my baby?

Joseph: It's your prerogative, but all I'm saying is either you get an abortion or prove in court that it's my baby. My blood type is so common that it's 25 percent of the whole U.S. population. So just as my man Johnny Cochran said in the O.J. Simpson case, "If it doesn't fit, you must acquit." If it's not in the blood, then it's not in the fatherhood. No blood, no father.

Renee: You low-down dirty dog. I thought you were different. Joseph: No baby, I'm like all the other brothers who have my blood type. If you can't prove in court that the baby is mine, then a man's got to do what a man's got to do. I mean how do I know that it's mine? You know the phrase, "mama's baby, papa maybe." I don't know who you've been with. I'm not with you all the time. I don't even know if you go to work everyday. I don't know what you do when you're not with me.

Father Fighting for Custody

Raymond was a fourth-grade elementary teacher. He had always loved working with children, and his mother, also a teacher, inspired him early in life to consider teaching as a profession. Later he committed to education when he read reports stating that most African American boys never experienced a male teacher of their own race in the elementary grades.

Diane, Raymond's wife of 10 years, was a buyer for a major department store. Traveling to New York and Paris on buying trips at least once a month, she thoroughly enjoyed her career. She was a country girl from rural Georgia who had made good in the hotly competitive fashion industry.

Although Raymond and Diane loved their jobs, the pressure of work and raising young twin boys had taken its toll on their marriage. Like so many other working couples, they ended up in divorce court. More than anything, Raymond wanted custody of his boys. His job was stable, he was professionally trained to work with children, and besides, he just naturally loved them. Diane also wanted custody, and she was sure that the judge would agree that as long as she was fit, the children belonged with their mother. When Raymond asked who would take care of them when she was traveling, she assured him that her mother would pitch in. Then she dropped the bomb that no loving parent ever wants to hear: she announced that she was planning to move to New York in order to cut down her traveling schedule. She knew she could convince her supervisor to cut down on her international travel too.

Raymond knew that the American system of justice makes it very difficult for men to take custody of their children. He became distraught over the possibility of his sons moving to New York. At best, he'd have only a week or two during the summer with them. In addition, he'd have to pay $1,000 a month in child support. It wasn't fair.

"What can I do?" he asked his lawyer. "I love my boys. I believe boys need to be with their father. Why do the courts feel that I'm not the better parent? What criteria do they use? Is it because she makes more money than me? Well, I work fewer hours than she does. I have more time to spend with them. Not only that, I have my summers off. That's our time to go fishing - Diane doesn't even like to fish or play basketball. Who's going to teach them how to defend themselves?" The lawyer remained silent, listening sympathetically. He had heard this story many times before. "It's not fair that I have to send $12,000 a year and only see my boys two weeks during the summer. There has to be some way for me to get custody of my children!"

The Brother with the Weak Rap

Nicole was a sophomore in high school. She had just turned 15 and was number two in her class. Her career goal was to become a pediatrician. Everybody was proud of Nicole. Her grandmother and mother struggled to make ends meet, working whenever they could to pay the bills. They wanted things to be different for Nicole because she had been a good student throughout elementary school, and having just completed her first year of high school, things seemed to be continuing.

4

Nicole began to change during her adolescence. She wanted to wear her hair like the older girls. While her mother disapproved of her lipstick and makeup, because her mother left for work before she went to school, Nicole was always able to put a little on before she left for her first class.

Nicole had begun to change in other ways. No longer the skinny 88-pound freshman, Nicole was now a shapely 104-pound sophomore. The extra pounds seemed to all have fallen in just the right places. Her chest had begun to fill out and her behind and legs gave the impression that she was much older. Things were looking up for Nicole, not just her GPA, but also her physique. The brothers also discovered the changes. They no longer saw the nerd of her youth, but instead viewed Nicole as a young woman.

Although Nicole spent a lot of her time in school with her female and male nerd friends, who were in honor's classes, as soon as seventh period ended, she preferred walking home with a brother named Raynard. Raynard used to talk about her "like a dog" when she was younger. He had called her a little girl. Raynard was the first to tell Nicole that she had grown up. Raynard was 19 and could have any lady he wanted. He had everything that any sister on the block could imagine. He was 6'4", fine, drove a black Mustang and always had money in his pocket. Sometimes he got his money dealing drugs on the corner and sometimes he earned it with his part-time stock job. Everybody knew that his being a stock clerk was merely a cover.

Raynard had decided that school was not for him and had dropped out in his junior year. He knew how to rap and make a lady feel important. His next conquest

5

was Nicole. Unfortunately, Nicole never graduated from high school nor enrolled in college or medical school. She never achieved her goal of becoming a doctor. She did make it to the hospital, but as a patient. She made it there at least five times to give birth. Nicole now has five babies and Raynard is gone. Nicole got caught by a brother with a weak rap. For if Raynard possessed a stronger rap, he would have sought women his own age.

Single Parenting

5:30 a.m. The alarm clock awakens Keisha to another grueling day. This 18-year-old single mother dresses and feeds herself and her son Kojo. On Mondays, Wednesdays, and Fridays, she goes to the local junior college. Fortunately, childcare is available at the school. Keisha also wants to work full time, but finding a position that fits her time, benefits, and salary needs is difficult.

Since Keisha can't afford to support herself or Kojo, she still lives with her mother. She plans to move into her own apartment in a year. Sometimes Grandma helps with childcare, but not often. She believes that if Keisha was grown enough to lay down with a man and have a baby, then she is grown enough to assume responsibility for childcare. She is very firm on the point and refuses to allow Keisha to take advantage of her.

When Keisha's mother first learned of Keisha's pregnancy, she had been very disappointed. It had happened during her daughter's junior year in high school. She was so young! Not only has she kept her promise, she is now taking three classes at the local junior college. Her mother is proud of her tenacity toward getting a college education. Keisha has won back her respect.

Keisha is determined not become another statistic on the welfare rolls. She really wants a job, so her mother has agreed to help her with Kojo two days during the week. She finally found a part-time data entry job paying minimum wage, but she is happy to be working. Keisha wants to work longer hours to make more money, and she could, if only her supervisor would let her keep Kojo with her while she worked. He refused, but recommended a preschool four blocks from the office. Unfortunately, $40.00 per week on Keisha's salary is financially prohibitive.

Nearly every day finds Keisha begging one of her girlfriends to keep Kojo beyond her mother's commitment. Kojo's father appears about three time a year—on Kojo's birthday, Christmas, and Father's Day—so he's no help. Keisha calls him a "holiday father." She's learned the hard way that children need their parents every day.

Father Laid Off

Bernard and Catherine had been married for 12 years. It had been a typical marriage with the typical peaks and valleys, but they had weathered the storms, unlike many of their friends who had divorced. They had grown closer over the years. They had a moderately sized house in the city and had four beautiful children, two boys and two girls. They felt blessed that the Lord had given them their heart's desires.

7

Bernard had always been a good provider. Despite only having a high school diploma, he was fortunate to work on an assembly line of a manufacturing company. Because he had a good work ethic and followed directions, he did well on his job, avoided downsizing and continued being promoted because of his excellent workstyle. While Catherine had two years of college, Bernard was still earning more and their combined salaries made them middle class.

Bernard and Catherine often laughed at being considered middle class because they said they didn't feel like it and the checkbook didn't reflect it. They used to often tease each other and say "if we're middle class, we're hanging on by the threads cause if one of us ever misses a paycheck, we will leave this class and go to the lower class." Unfortunately, that realization became a reality.

Bernard's company was having financial problems with overseas competitors, whose factories were modernized and more productive. The company decided that the only way to compete was to close its U.S. plants and open a plant in Eastern Asia.

Catherine has become more and more worried about Bernard. He used to come home straight after work and play with his children. Now Bernard doesn't come home till 11:00 at night or later. It seems like he always comes home after the children are asleep. She wonders if Bernard is embarrassed about not being able to provide for his children. Catherine begins to cry, thinking about last week when their older son asked Bernard for money to buy new Nike gym shoes. Bernard broke down and cried, explaining to his son that he didn't have the money. His daughter overheard the conversation. She hugged him and said, "Daddy that's okay, we still love you." But it didn't stop Bernard from crying. Catherine has been encouraging Bernard to look for work elsewhere, but she's not totally sure he's doing that. Bernard keeps complaining, who's going to hire a 42-year-old man with a high school diploma and pay him $14.35 an hour?

Catherine is worried because her husband is now spending more time on the streets drinking and may become the victim of random violence or begin to use harder drugs and/or become sexually promiscuous and catch some sexually transmittable disease. She is fearful of losing her husband. She had never been concerned about world affairs and the global economy. She smiled and snickered to herself because she could barely remember the relationship between Illinois, Michigan and Indiana, much less world geography. Her marriage was now affected by world geography, the global economy and monopoly capitalism. She fell asleep after midnight waiting for Bernard.

When Will We Learn?

Barbara was 20 and the mother to five children ranging from infancy to seven. Unfortunately, each baby had a different father. Barbara used to always sit around the house complaining to her friends about her station in life and trifling Black men. She said she was too young to be held back by these five hardheaded children. Barbara said that she needed to party and to make something of herself. But how was she going to do this with five children?

Sometimes she would express her frustration in front of her children. The children would look at her, and, without saying it, remind her it was not their volition to come into the world at this time through her. At other times, Barbara would blame the five men that had fathered her children, and the five to ten other men that she had been sexually involved with over the years for being irresponsible and self-centered. She said it was their behavior that had left her in this horrendous and precarious position. Having once read that opposites attract led Barbara to believe that she was a good woman who deserved better. Her problem was she was attracting people with different values - she needed to become involved with someone positive like herself.

A girlfriend had just given her a copy of Iyanla Vanzant's book, *Acts of Faith*. She had read that opposites don't attract and that your mate is a reflection of who you are. Barbara now ponders her future. What is a 20-year-old African American woman going to do with five children by five different fathers who are not involved in their child's growth and development? What man would come into her life and actively get involved in the nurturing and development of five children that did not belong to him?

What are the implications to Barbara if welfare legislation is altered, creating maximum limits on the number of children and the number of years that a child can receive welfare? Barbara continues to look out the window and reflects on those years between 13 and 20. During those years no one could tell her anything. While she was looking fine on the outside, internally she struggled with very serious issues.

Homicide

It was a hot summer day and Pat was cleaning the kitchen when she heard three gunshots. Unfortunately, in her neighborhood, over the years that sound had become the norm. Sometimes it was boys who were simply shooting in the air. Regretfully, though, there were other times when they were shooting at each other. Pat tried hard to make sure her two sons were in the house before dark. That goal became more difficult as the boys reached adolescence. Her older son was 14, and the youngest was 12. She often felt that she lived in a war zone. She once read that more African American males were killed in the inner city in one year than in the entire history of the Vietnam War or by the Ku Klux Klan.

Whenever she heard gunshots, she sent up a prayer, when she knew her two sons were in the house. But because this had been a hot summer day and they were older, she had let them play outside just a little longer this evening. So Pat did more than send up a prayer when she heard the three gunshots. She went to the front door to see if she could assess what had happened. She saw further down the block that a crowd had formed and they were looking down at someone.

Suddenly, one of the girls on the block ran to her and said, Ms. Butler, your older son has been shot. Pat's legs began to wobble. Her arms wanted to rush out and go down the street, but her legs were numb. Finally, out of shock she ran down the street with the young girl, hollering and screaming. Her younger son was standing over his brother crying. He looked up and saw his mom and said, "he's dead. My brother is dead." Pat looked around the eyes of the crowd and asked "who did it?" Everybody seemed to look the other way. The police cars finally arrived, along with an ambulance.

Over the next few days and weeks Pat will be involved with the police department and the funeral home. She will have one son left. What happens to a family that's been victimized by violence? What happens to a mother who loses her child? What does violence do to the surviving children in a family?

Can Anything Good Come Out of Nazareth?

Ben Carson was nine years of age. He was failing fourth grade and his mother knew that he could do better. They were a poor family. They were a single-parent family and Ms. Carson only had a third grade education. She knew that Ben had potential and was a gifted student, but she didn't know what to do. She had talked with his teachers over the past two or three years and they all agreed that Ben had potential. They said he was a little hyperactive and became bored in class. The teachers always seemed to put the burden on Ms. Carson and asked about the environment at home. What could she say? Other than the truth - we were poor, but always had enough food to eat and clothes to wear.

Ms. Carson's older sister, who had a couple years of college, had suggested to her that the boys needed to read more and watch television less. Ms. Carson decided she would have them read a book weekly and write a paper that her sister would review to make sure that it reflected the contents of the book. Ms. Carson had reared her household on the major principle: *A family that prays together stays together.* At family devotion one Sunday night after church, she announced that starting on Monday there would not be any television during the week. The boys could play for an hour, but they had to read a book and write a report weekly.

Ben was furious at this new protocol. He whined to his mother asking why he had to do this. "You're going to turn us into sissies." No one else on the block was denied television and made to read. Ms. Carson had to remind them, you don't belong to the other parents on the block, you belong to me. It was very difficult at the beginning for her to get her two sons to read. Often, they would fall asleep because they said they were bored. She noticed however, that their grades began to improve and eventually their attitude about reading began to change. Ben now said he liked reading because he traveled around the world and met all types of people he had never known of before. He especially liked reading about animals and rocks. Often he was able to make special contributions to class discussions because of a book he had read outside of class.

Even though some of his friends began to think he was a little nerdy, he felt good about his teacher's approval and encouragement to read more. Ben became one of the best students in his elementary school and continued his success into high school and college.

He became a neurosurgeon and today is considered one of the best in his field. "Can anything good come from Nazareth?" The best neurosurgeon in the country came from inner city Detroit, from a low-income, single-parent household, with a mother who possessed a third-grade education.

Spousal Abuse

Willie and Diane really loved each other. They were high school sweethearts and married three years after they had graduated from high school at age 20. Six years later they were still madly in love with each other. Madly literally. It was Diane's big mouth that made Willie hit her. It was Willie's bad temper that caused all the problems. No matter who was at fault, Willie was never too angry to enjoy the make up after break up.

Makeup was exactly what Diane needed after a round with Willie-Mike Tyson. Her pretty face of 26 had become a weather-beaten face of 40. Her family was right: no hitting man only hits once.

Finally, Diane listened to her family and asked Willie to get counseling. "I don't need a quack telling me how to act. I need a woman who knows when to keep her mouth shut." Diane countered, "I need a man who can control himself. If the frustrations on the job are causing all this turmoil, why don't you take it out on the people who are causing you this grief? Why take it out on a 5'1", 107-pound wife who loves you? And how is it that you can control your temper all day until you get home to me and then lose it?

This last brawl had been pretty serious. Diane was in intensive care suffering from a concussion while Willie was waiting in the hospital lobby. Willie began to sob because Diane was all he had. While he was sobbing in the lobby, he turned and saw Diane's parents walking through the hospital doors. Embarrassed, he buried his head in his hands.

Blended Families

It was Saturday afternoon. This was going to be the big day. David and Crystal had been dating for almost six months. They were both in their early thirties and had been previously married. David's two children by his first wife were with him every other weekend. Crystal's two children lived with her. Because she was very concerned about exposing them to her dates, she'd vow to herself that her significant other would not interact with her children until the relationship had grown and developed into a stable one.

She thought six months was an appropriate time to take it to another level. This particular summer afternoon represented that six-months experience. David and Crystal had planned to meet with both sets of children and have a picnic in the park, where they were going to have a real nice lunch, enjoying volleyball, softball and whatever else the children desired. It was going to be a very interesting gathering because Crystal had two girls and David had two boys. Crystal had always been concerned about exposing her daughters to another man. David's boys had an undying love for their mother. They were devoted to her and David knew it would be a real challenge for Crystal to make an inroad into their hearts.

They both knew that in order to stay together they were going to have to blend the two families, and today was going to be the start of the thousand-mile journey. Crystal and David had talked about the complexity of blended families. They had discussed how they wanted to be addressed by each other's children. They had also pondered about what would happen when David's children came over. Would there be enough room in the house? They had even begun planning meals. David and the boys were vegetarians while Crystal and the girls ate everything but pork.

They often discussed how their ex-spouses would respond, react, and possibly interfere in this new blended family. Today they were simply going to implement their theory and enjoy the picnic. As David began to prepare to go over to Crystal's house, he prayed that her girls would like him. Simultaneously, across town, Crystal was praying that David's boys would not compare her to their mother.

Adultery

Darryl and Linda had been married for ten years. They had three children. They had a beautiful house, two cars, were a two career family, and attended church most Sundays. The children went to private schools and wore braces. On Saturdays time was spent between dance class, gymnastics, and martial arts. Everybody said they were the ideal couple, but Darryl knew that was a lie.

Five years ago he and one of his staff members who worked on projects together began an affair. Darryl felt that Judy really understood him in a way that Linda never had. When he would come home from work it seemed that Linda spent more time talking about the children, making dinner, washing dishes and checking homework and that there was very little time left for them. Worse still, Linda was an early morning person, which also meant she went to bed earlier in the evening, and Darryl was a night owl and often stayed up until after midnight. Also, Darryl was an engineer, and because of the technical nature of his work, when he'd attempt to talk with her about his challenges, Linda didn't seem to grasp the concepts and this frustrated him further.

Darryl felt that Judy understood him because she was his assistant. She was also the most beautiful woman he had ever met. During the five-year affair, Judy had always said that because of the male shortage, she didn't want all of his time, just some of it. She knew going into the relationship that he was already married and that his family came first. Judy said that all she ever wanted was his friendship, respect, and one date a week ending with one weekly uninhibited   passionate lovemaking.

David initially agreed, but it was becoming more difficult. It was becoming more of a strain to come home and talk about the selection of new furniture, buying new carpet, and what the girls needed for school. He found himself thinking more about Judy and wanting to spend more than one night a week with her. He didn't know what to do. He knew what he wanted to do on a physical level, but he was very concerned about his career and public opinion. He didn't know if he could afford child support. He also knew he could not look Linda in the eye and say that for the last five years they'd been living a lie. Linda had asked him the day before about taking a three-day vacation to the Bahamas. He immediately thought how great the trip would be with Judy. Ironic isn't it, that these thoughts are rushing through his mind as he's about to receive the "Family Man of the Year Award" at their children's school. His wife and three children lead the applause as he prepares to give an acceptance speech.

Drug Abuse

Doug and Elaine have been married for seven years. Doug was the introvert and Elaine was the extrovert. They were happily married and decided not to have any children. Their frequent partying included drinking and smoking. They enjoyed each other's company and could party from 11 p.m. until 4:00 a.m. Because they hated seeing people sloppy drunk, they were quite skilled at monitoring their intake.

Over the years it appeared they had it under control. They had a nice house, luxurious cars and wardrobes that spilled into the remaining closets. Elaine often teased Doug, saying the reason we don't have any children is because we had to use their closets for our additional clothes.

Over the past year, alcohol had become not enough for Doug. He said he didn't like the way it felt in his stomach and it affected his digestion; he wanted a greater high than alcohol could give. He had tried reefer in college and now every once in a while he smoked a couple of joints. He said marijuana never gave him the ultimate high. Elaine knew something had happened because this year Doug, for some reason, decided to have his own checking account.

Doug found his ecstasy in the "white powder." It made him forget about why he wasn't promoted on his job. It made him forget about the cruelty of being Black in White America. He felt life was very mundane. You work five days, play two days, and two weeks of the year you get a chance to enjoy a vacation. Elaine also noticed fluctuations in Doug's sexual potency. In bed sometimes he was great and other times nothing happened.

She asked him if he was using cocaine. Although Doug never answered her directly, he gave the same answer he'd always given about alcohol, "I have it under control."

Elaine was startled by the ringing of the telephone. When she answers the phone, the hospital administrator tells her that Doug is in the emergency room, that he blacked out at the wheel and that the police said that he'd been under the influence.

The "Cosby Show" Reality

Walter and Jackie are celebrating their silver anniversary. The Lord has been good to them. They have been married for 25 years, have four beautiful children who either are in college or have graduated and Walter and Jackie are two years away from retirement. He's been a pastor of a local church and the principal at the high school for the past 15 years. His wife Jackie has been the choir director and a pediatrician.

They've had their peaks and valleys over the years. One of the children had a serious bout with asthma. Jackie's mother lived with them for 10 years before she died. Jackie literally brings all of her cases home to talk about at the dinner table. Walter has been equally guilty of wanting to bring home every way-ward child. It's also been challenging developing, maintaining and nurturing a local church.

Tonight is their 25th anniversary and the four children and two grandchildren are present. Friends and other family members from around the area have come to celebrate this joyous occasion with this beautiful family.

The grandchildren want them to hurry and cut the cake, but the adults are hollering "Speech, speech, speech!" Walter, who's never been short on words, says "God has been good to us. He's been better to us than we have been to ourselves. We could have gone our separate ways. We had plenty of excuses that could have driven us in that direction. We come from a long tradition of families that have stayed together. My parents and grandparents stayed together. The same is true for Jackie. We also felt our children deserved to see a couple that could resolve their differences. God is good, all the time! Now, let's cut the cake."

CHAPTER TWO

THE FIRST GENERATION

The Lord will let the people be governed by immature boys. Everyone will take advantage of everyone else. Young people will not respect their elders and worthless people will not respect their superiors.
Isaiah 3:4-5.   *Good News Translation*

African people have an exceptional history, having been the first people on earth almost four million years ago, living in the southeastern part of Africa. It was in Africa that African people developed the laws of medicine, science, math, language arts, and religion. Other people from around the world, Romans, Greeks, Asians, Arabs, have all come to Africa initially to learn the culture, but ultimately to steal and call it theirs. It is amazing how some European scholars argue that in that era of history, 2800 B.C., when the pyramids were being built, this civilization was populated by a multi-racial society.

The obvious question should be, if Europeans had developed a technology to heat iron at high temperatures, built a pyramid 48 stories high, 755 feet wide, with 2,300,000 stones, each weighing three tons, being perfectly balanced and right-angled, shouldn't we see remnants of that technology and development in Greece or Rome during the same era? The only explaination of how these advancements could reside exclusively in Africa during that era is that the developers were African people.

As you read this chapter, the trends and rumors in the African American family are alarming and inconsistent with the African tradition.

This is the first generation of African American youth that may not exceed their parents in academic achievement.

Every generation of African American youth has exceeded their parents in academic achievement. During slavery, African people were denied the opportunity to read. Many enslaved Africans were whipped if they were caught reading. Their desire to read was so strong and intense that many of them defied those consequences and continued to read by candlelight. In 1930, 65 years after chattel slavery, only 20 percent of the African American population was illiterate. By contrast, in 2000 functional illiteracy had risen to 44 percent.[1]

How could a people that built the first civilization and that has a track record of every generation exceeding the previous generation in academic achievement, now enter into an era where the current generation will be the first that will not exceed their parents? Could this also be the first generation of parents who have given their children their own telephone, television, VCR, stereo system, CD player, Nintendo, Sega

Genesis and similar gadgets in their room? Could African American parents be giving their children more things than time? I've even observed that in lower-income families, children seem to have the most expensive pair of gym shoes, starter jackets and Walkmans, but may not have $10 worth of school supplies.

Before desegregation, African American teachers required children to do their best and would not allow them to pass to the next grade without demonstrating competency. After integration, we have teachers who allow students to pass to the next grade without minimal, if any, improvement.

I ask schools why they believe in "social promotion." They offer flimsy excuses such as we don't want a 11-year-old boy sitting in a classroom with 6-year-old students. Some are more honest and indicate that it's simply too costly for the school district to educate a child for more years than what is required.

It's unfortunate that we feel it's cheaper to send a person to prison, spending from $18,000 to $38,000 per year rather than retaining a child in first grade at a cost of $6,000. In addition, I believe that we can save $6,000 if we hold teachers accountable for 180 days and six hours per day. I'm still naive enough to believe, along with Asa Hilliard, Barbara Sizemore, Jerome Harris, and Marva Collins, that if you give me 180 days and six hours per day, I will show you a minimum of one year advancement in reading and math.

Literacy could be the greatest challenge to the African American family. The burden of education should not be solely on the school system. African

American parents need to teach their children how to read and not allow them to be promoted for social and financial reasons. How can a parent not know that their ten-year-old child can't read? Research indicates that the majority of African American inmates have a poor academic background.[2] We could reduce our incarceration figures by increasing literacy. It becomes crucial between kindergarten and fourth grade that African American children become literate. If not, they may never become self-actualized adults.

This is the first generation where elders are now afraid of children.

In the early 1990's in St. Louis and again in 1995 in Chicago, there were tremendous heat waves where temperatures soared passed 100 degrees. Both cities attempted to provide assistance for elders, who in many cases were in facilities without proper ventilation, fans or air conditioning. Many elders chose to keep their doors and windows closed rather than taking the risk of opening them and being attacked by children who have no respect for life.

I am still grappling with how over 500 people died in Chicago during that record-breaking summer of 1995. Many elders chose hunger rather than chance walking to the corner store and possibly being mugged and robbed by children. In the African tradition, children are the reward of life and elders are the most respected. I believe a major determinant in measuring the viability of a people is how well they respect their elders. In the African tradition, I'm not even allowed to speak without seeking permission from an elder.

Some mothers will choose crack over their children.

It has been said of this world where change has become the norm, there are very few things that are stable and constant. Historically, there were two things you could always count on: The Lord and African American mothers. It had been said that nothing could separate African American mothers from their children. African women held onto their babies in the dungeon, on the slave ship, the plantation and mass migrations north. But there is something that can separate African American mothers from their children and it's crack cocaine.

Research indicates that 84 percent of female drug users are of childbearing ages.[3] I have seen mothers leave their children for hours and days for crack. I have witnessed mothers forget they had children. Black women have now been seen performing sexual acts in front of their children to secure crack cocaine. What makes the matter especially frightening is that the majority of the time it has been African American males who made her addicted, by giving it to her free initially. As the gospel songstress Helen Baylor says, "How many of you know it wasn't for free?" What makes this issue more complex is the unanswered question: What is society to do with crack-addicted babies?

Some children have never seen a family member work.

Can you imagine living in a building where no one works? Living in a family where no one works? A family where two or three generations have participated in "Mother's Day," which is the first of the month, when mothers go to the post office and pick up their welfare checks?

Before integration, African American children could live in a family where no one worked, but they could look down the hall or down the block and observe other adults working as bus drivers, teachers and doctors. They all lived in close proximity to each other. After integration, the village lost some of its best role models and the concentration of poverty increased.

Julius Wilson, in his book *The Truly Disadvantaged,* describes one of the largest public housing developments in the country, the Robert Taylor Homes in Chicago. It is a complex of 28 16-story buildings covering 92 acres. The official population was almost 20,000, but according to a recent report there are an additional 5,000 to 7,000 adult residents who are not registered with the housing authority. All of the registered households were Black and 69 percent of the official population were minors. The median family income was $5,470, and 93 percent of the children lived with a single parent. Eighty-three percent of the families with children received Aid to the Family for Dependent Children (AFDC).[4]

The opening scripture of this chapter relating the Lord's allowing the people to be governed by immature boys sounds almost like a current newspaper describing conditions in many parts of the African American community, and specifically in these housing developments. We have buildings that are populated with women and children, where only 7 percent of the residents are adult males. Unfortunately, young boys between the ages of 11 and 19 believe they are in charge. They believe they are the men of the building.

The concentration of poverty becomes pathological. An exhaustive study of poverty and the impact for future generations by Oscar Lewis lays the foundation for the conceptual limitation of cycles of poverty. According to Lewis,

> The crucial thing about the subculture of poverty is that it represents both the reaction and an adaptation of the poor to the marginality and helplessness in the larger society. The subcultural poverty is specific to capitalist society, in which the marginalized, illiterate, slum dwelling poor develop a way of life that is passed down from generation to generation along family lines. Although this subcultural poverty may begin as an adaptation to the highest conditions of poverty, it becomes a culture with a life of its own due to the socialization of children. Once it comes into existence it tends to perpetuate itself from generation to generation because of its effect on the children. By the time slum children are six or seven years old, they usually have absorbed the basic values and attitudes of their subcultures and are not psychologically geared to take full advantage of changing conditions or increased opportunities which may occur in their lifetime.[5]

In the chapter, "Restoring the Village," I will be offering programs and solutions that are designed to break this cycle of poverty. This will not be an easy challenge. We must break the cycle of poverty before seven years of age and teach literacy before nine.

African Americans can't stay married.

In my book *The Power, Passion and Pain of Black Love*, I reported that the divorce rate in America is 50 percent and among African Americans it is now 66 percent.[6] I often tease people in my workshops and mention I will give them the book free if they can name five happily married unchurched couples under 45 years of age who have been married for at least seven years. Seldom do I have a winner.

Notice in that criterion that two of those factors were age and church involvement. Most of us could list five couples that are married over 45 years of age. That should teach us that our elders must know something that we don't know about the secret of staying together. The current narcissism that exists in our society, where people feel unfulfilled and have to leave their mate and "fly to Seattle" to find themselves exists more with our youth than our elders.

Second, I excluded church involvement. Couples who are saved, pray together, read scripture and worship together have a divorce ratio of 1:244.[7] Much more will be mentioned in the following chapter on love and commitment. In this chapter we're looking at trends and rumors that are frightening to the very existence of the African American family. Why is it so difficult to stay married in America? Why is the divorce rate lower in "third world" countries and much higher in "first world" America?

African Americans don't know their neighbors.

This is the first generation of African American parents who are trying to raise their children by themselves. Many believe they can raise their children without the input and assistance from their neighbors.

In previous generations, African Americans did not assume they could work downtown, come home, lock the door, watch television and raise their children by themselves. I also challenge members of my workshop by offering them the book, *To Be Popular or Smart: The Black Peer Group*, if they could name five of their children's friends, their parents, their address and phone number. Can you? Can you do it without looking in your phone book?

Parents will curse their child's teacher.

Teachers used to be very respected figures in America. They remain revered and respected in Africa, Japan and Germany. Civilized countries realized that whatever you want to be in this world, i.e., computer programmer, lawyer, doctor it will require being taught by a teacher. I encourage college students to pursue majoring in education because we may be one of the few groups asking someone else to educate our children.

In 2000, we were 17 percent of the public school student population and 8 percent of the teachers. By the year 2010, African American students will be 25 percent of the students and only 5 percent of the teachers.[8] In the past, teachers and parents were on the same side. They often lived in the same neighborhood. They knew each other and had mutual respect. Unfortunately, most teachers no longer live in the neighborhood in which they teach. Parents are younger and more insecure and will often believe their children's version of the story without seeking the teacher's version before they curse them. Many young people tell me that they don't want to teach because of the lack of respect from both student and parent. Many teachers when referring to themselves say "I'm just a teacher." Many educators have now become afraid of both students and parents. I wonder what parents expect from their children after their child has witnessed them cursing the teacher? Do parents really expect their child to respect the teacher henceforth? Do they really feel the teachers will continue to work hard, provide high expectations and a nurturing environment for their child? Will the child leave this scenario feeling that he or she has won and this can be replicated throughout the entire year?

Some African American men call women Bs.

An excellent way to measure the viability of a culture is to observe how men treat women. Another effective way to measure is to listen to the lyrics. Some of our best musical griots are James Brown and Gil Scott-Heron, none of whom refers to Black women as Bs. Gil Scott-Heron's cassette *Spirits* tells the current rappers that they can't call her a B in one song and a queen in the other. Something is wrong with people who refer to women as "Bs." Something is equally wrong with women who respond to that salutation. It is absolutely pathetic for an African American woman to buy a rapper's cassette to hear herself being called a B.

I won't live to see my 21st birthday.

It's very difficult selling youth on long-term gratification when they aren't confident they'll live to see tomorrow. To believe in the American dream, which suggests graduating from college will generate a good job in their field of study and a three-bedroom suburban house, is not a fathomable reality for many African Americans. Education and employment are based on these long-term values.

We now live in a society, specifically in the African American community, where grandparents are burying their grandchildren. It used to be isolated cases that parents had to bury their children, but seldom did you observe grandparents burying their grandchildren. We now have children who have little or no value for life. In my earlier book, *Hip Hop versus MAAT*, I described a killing exercise. Boys gave 37 reasons why they would kill someone including, he ate one of my french fries, he stepped on my shoe, he looked at me funny and said hello to my lady, etc.

In my work with young people nationwide, the most challenging issue I have to face is how to respond to a young person who is convinced that it would be better to drive a BMW for three months and then die, rather than live a longer life, but either have to take a bus or drive a Chevrolet. Our ancestors struggled in the dungeon, slave ships and plantations. They endured the worst holocaust ever experienced, but remained confident they would live to see their 21st birthday. They were more confident in life expectancy than this generation.

Where are the fathers?

There is a rumor that by the year 2050, there will be no African American fathers living with their children. In 1920, 90 percent of our children had their fathers at home. In 1960, 80 percent of our children had their fathers at home. In 2002, only 32 percent of our children had their fathers at home.[9] With this current trend, by the year 2000 there will be less than 30 percent and by the year 2050 there may not be *one* African American family that has its father present.

Many daughters have never been hugged by their fathers.

The first love a girl should receive from a male should her father's. Can you imagine a fatherless Black America? We need to ask ourselves what we can offer to refute the current trend. What can we postulate to refute the trend that fatherlessness will increase? In a subsequent chapter, we will probe this phenomenon in more detail.

Many African American children lack basic home training.

This is the first generation of African American youth who have not been taught to take their hats off when they're in a building. They have not been taught how to keep their pants from falling down. This is the first generation of African American youth who have not been taught basic words such as *thank you, please, excuse me, good morning, hello, good bye* and *I'm sorry.* We now have a generation of African American youth who will interrupt two adults who are speaking to each other without saying excuse me. We have African American youth who have been given something and have not been taught to say *thank you.*

We have African American youth who will eat a meal, and not know the purpose of a knife, fork or spoon. When I worked as a youth counselor in a residential facility, I observed African American children who would never use a knife and fork and the majority of the time they used their hands and at best, used a spoon. I witnessed dinners inclusive of meat, potatoes, vegetables and bread where invariably, whatever the meal was, the children would always convert it to a sandwich, because that's what they were accustomed to eating.

My father used to often remind me if you only have one pair of pants, make sure they're clean and ironed before you wear them again. Many African American families taught their children you may have been born in the ghetto, but the ghetto does not live in you. We now are experiencing the first generation of African American youth who have not been taught basic grooming habits. The real tragedy is that they have become parents and the lack of home training continues.

Some parents are afraid of their children.

It is hard for me to imagine a parent bringing a child into the world and then telling another adult nine years later they don't know what to do with him or her. Many parents are afraid of their children. I still know fifty-year-old mothers who stand a mere 4'1" and can tell their 6'1" sons who are 20 years of age, "I brought you in here and I will take you out." I don't believe we lose our children at 13 to 18 years of age. This is also the first generation where the children are paying the bills. Some parents have no qualms with their drug dealing sons paying the rent, utility, food and other necessities.

It seems as if the ends justify the means. This is also the first generation of parents who no longer query what their children bring home. There used to be a time when the parents took the position that if you didn't buy those gym shoes, pants, shirt, jacket, cap or jewelry you couldn't bring it home. Some children can now wear a $70 cap, a $100 pair of gym shoes, $200 sweatsuits, and $300 gold chains, with no questions asked. I remember when I was growing up my parents used to often tease me saying, "I sent you to school with $69.95 from your cap to your shoes and that's what I expect you to bring home."

I propose the critical age for most of our problems is between six and nine years of age and began when the parent told the child to empty the garbage and the child did not move until the eighth time, when the parent threatened him or her with the skillet. It bothers me when I see parents curse their children, but it's equally infuriating when I see children curse their parents. I believe that we have a dangerous time bomb on our hands when parents cannot control their children. What are we expecting of teachers when parents lose control?

That's my daddy.

This is the first generation where African American children are in a class where there are three children in the class with different mothers, but the same father. "That's my daddy," says the child. "No it's not, that's my daddy." "No it's not, that's my daddy." All three children were correct. These three five-year-old kindergarten children were very excited to see their father come into the building. While the three children had different mothers, what they all had in common was the same father.

I would love to dialog with one of these "sperm donors" and try to understand psychologically how it happened. I wonder about the psychological state of the three children. They didn't know before they went to kindergarten they had another sibling. I wonder if the father will treat them as siblings and take them to the park. I also wonder about the three mothers and how they feel about this one man. Can you imagine the mothers finding out from their children? It's the first generation where African American children had the same daddy but different mothers in the same class.

Drug dealers employ more African Americans than the Black middle class.

I wonder how W. E. B. DuBois would have felt about the contributions of the Talented Tenth. There is no group of Africans anywhere in the world, including Nigeria and Brazil, who have more Africans with degrees than Africans living in America. Two million Africans have degrees in the United States with presently 1.3 million enrolled in college.[10] Unfortunately because most schools teach how to become employees and not employers, most African Americans seek employment over entrepreneurship.

Many African American males who were expelled from the school system without pencil, paper or calculator can convert kilos to grams and grams to dollar bills. They seem to understand marketing and collections equally well. These drug dealing brothers without a high school diploma employ more African Americans than the Black middle class, specifically African American males. Where are educated African Americans employing African American males?

I don't believe in God.

This is the first generation where many African American youth do not have a personal relationship with the Lord. Author C. Eric Lincoln describes an increasingly "unchurched" youth generation.[11] This is the first generation of African American youth who will not pray before eating.

The church is no longer viewed as a sacred place in the neighborhood. We now have a generation of youth who will rob the church. Many pastors employ security guards, not only throughout the week but during their worship service. Many pastors have to remind their congregations to take their purses and other valuable possessions to the alter, because after prayer, your possessions may no longer be on the pew.

Throughout the book, we will be attempting to provide solutions to these frightening and alarming trends that are affecting the African American family. These trends were not designed to discourage, but were designed as a wake up call that our race is in trouble—and this is the reason why I've written this book. For the hour has drawn near, there is not much time left to save the African family. Solutions are offered in the following chapter on love, commitment and marriage.

CHAPTER THREE

LOVE, COMMITMENT, AND MARRIAGE

 enesis 2:18. *And the Lord God said it is not good that man should be alone. I will make him a helper, comparable to him.*

Genesis 2:22-24. *Then the rib which the Lord God had taken from man, He made into a woman and He brought her to the man, and Adam said, this is now bone of my bones and flesh of my flesh. She shall be called woman because she was taken out of man. Therefore a man shall leave his father and mother and be joined to his wife. And they shall become one flesh.*

2 Corinthians 6:14. *Do not be unequally yoked together with unbelievers. For what fellowship has righteousness with lawlessness? And what communion has light with darkness?*

1 Corinthians 6:18. *Flee sexual immorality. Every sin the man does is outside the body. But he who commits immorality sins against his own body.*

Proverbs 6:32. *Whoever commits adultery with a woman lacks understanding. He who does so destroys his own soul.*

Luke 6:48. *He is like a man building a house who dug deep and laid the foundation on the rock. And when the flood arose, the stream beat vehemently against that house and could not shake it for it was founded on the rock.*

Ephesians 5:21-28. *Submitting to one another in the fear of God. Wives submit to your own husband as to your Lord. For the husband is head of the wife as also Christ is the head of the church and He is the Savior of the body. Therefore, just as the church is subject to Christ, so let the wives be to their own husband in everything. Husbands love your wives just as Christ also loved the Church and gave Himself for her, that He might sanctify and cleanse her with the washing of water by the word, that He might present to her to Himself a glorious church not having a spot or wrinkle or any such a thing, but that she should be holy and without blemish. So, husbands ought to want to love their own wives as their own bodies; he who loves his wife loves himself.*

Malachi 2:16. *For the Lord God of Israel says that He hates divorce.*

Good News Translation

I believe this is one of the most important chapters in the book and should precede fatherhood, motherhood and childhood, because the other three in an ideal, Godly, natural state occur after love, marriage, and commitment. A great deal of time and attention has gone into the selection of these scriptures.

I fundamentally believe that a family who digs deep by praying and reading the scriptures and places their house on Jesus will weather the storms. While the divorce rate previously mentioned is 50 percent for all Americans and 66 percent for African Americans, the divorce rate becomes one of 244 if they pray, read scripture, worship and both confess that Jesus is Lord of their lives.

Is it surprising that the United States leads the world in teen pregnancy? African American females are first and White American girls are third among all teenagers worldwide.[1] A recent study indicates that 70 percent of Americans think it's okay to have sex outside of marriage. Teen pregnancy in the African American community has reached epidemic proportion with almost 70 percent of our children born out of wedlock.[2] The Bible says to flee sexual immorality because it sins against our own body.

There are many obstacles facing the African American community. They include racism, sexism, monopoly capitalism, an inadequate educational system, lack of spirituality, values, self-hatred, lack of health care, drugs and violence. Some of these issues are external while others are internal, and the big debate between opposing groups, e.g. Democrats and Republicans, liberals and conservatives, integrationists and nationalists, is waged with limited resources; which should be emphasized—external or internal factors? This book, and specifically this chapter, is not designed to reintroduce that debate, but it is my desire to accentuate how significant teen pregnancy and out-of-wedlock conception have become in the African American community.

This problem cannot be exclusively blamed on racism. There is such a strong correlation between teen pregnancy, out-of-wedlock conception and other social ills that literally, if I had one request for the African American family, it would be abstinence outside of marriage. Can you imagine if African American families followed just that one basic prescription, that you can no longer have sex until marriage? Like the song says, "what a wonderful world this would be."

We now live in a society where many of us, including African Americans, belittle the impact of God's word and believe that it's old fashioned, unapplicable, and insignificant as we near the twenty-first century. Why does America lead the world in teen pregnancy? Could our media and lack of morals contribute to this epidemic? My first response is that the content and influence of rappers, talk shows, and soap operas, as well as elements sometimes found in barber and beauty shops, locker rooms, movies, bars and night clubs are detrimental for marital stability. If for no other reason, we should try God because it's obvious that the other sources are ineffective. Second and more importantly God's way has a better success rate and does not necessitate any grants, or new legislation, just *obedience*.

The consequence of out-of-wedlock conception should be obvious. The two sexual partners (notice I did not say adults) may never marry. The offspring may never live at home with both parents. The child may never receive spiritual, emotional and financial assistance.

The second area I want to highlight in this chapter is "being equally yoked." I believe that there are four stages in a relationship: *selection, romance, problem* and *commitment.* Many of us are in the problem stage because we did not follow God's prescription in stage one, the selection process.

Rather than relying on the Bible or our elders, we again invest ourselves in the opinions heard on the talk shows, soap operas, by rappers, barber shop, beauty shop, locker room and bar for a criterion on selecting a mate. We advertise our search in the classifieds and participate in radio talk shows indicating that we are looking for a mate that looks good, has a good sense of humor, is intelligent and wants to have a good time. Then wonder why the relationship lacks long-term commitment.

The problem should be obvious. If neither party believes that Jesus Christ is real, then that explains why being saved was not part of their selection criteria. Therefore, why ask God to save you in the finale, when He was not asked into the opening scene? The second dilemma occurs when at the outset, neither party believes that Jesus Christ is real, but one becomes saved during the marriage. First Corinthians 7:14 gives a charging response to the believer by saying "for the unbelieving husband is sanctified by the wife, and the unbelieving wife is sanctified by the husband; otherwise your children will be unclean but now they're holy." The responsibility of the believer is to remain. The unbeliever can part, but the believer is held responsible since the Lord hates divorce. The burden of the believer, having been saved after marriage, to live in a household with an unbeliever can be very challenging.

That's why it's very important *not* to get married until you know *whose* you are, and *who* you are. Your relationship with God and your identity need to be developed *before* marriage. Elders and adults have legitimate reasons why they prefer youth to delay their marital decisions. People who have not reconciled their relationship with God, have not internalized Africentricity, have not become economically and domestically self-sufficient, and have had limited dating experiences should delay marriage.

People who have not taken full responsibility for their happiness should delay marriage. When I review some of the classified ads for people looking for mates and talk to people about their desires, some of them say they *prefer* that the person be saved, which also says something about their own relationship with God. Anyone with a serious relationship with God no longer makes it a preference, but a prerequisite.

In my book *The Power, Passion and Pain of Black Love*, I said that selecting a mate is a science that begins with studying yourself. I believe the better you understand yourself, the greater success you'll have finding a mate. I also propose that if you are doing what you enjoy naturally, your spirit attracts like-minded people. If I was looking for a mate, I would focus on three things about myself that are extremely important, my relationship with the Lord, my commitment to the liberation of African people and my love for children. I would then place myself in these three environments and there's a probability that someone with similar interests will be attracted to me and vice versa.

Since the release of *The Power, Passion and Pain of Black Love,* I've received numerous letters from people telling me that my theory does not work. They attended church for the past four weeks and as of yet, still not met their mate! They have ignored—knowingly or unknowingly—my entire analysis. If you love the Lord, you are going to church anyway. Why are you now leaving the church simply because you haven't found a mate in four weeks. Often when we are *not* looking for a mate and doing those things we naturally enjoy, we create a serenity and joy that becomes contagious and attracts other people.

In spite of America's high divorce rate, it has not reduced our desire to enter another relationship. While America is against polygamy, serial marriages seem to be the American alternative. For others, "shacking" has become the norm. Some have lived with in excess of ten different mates. In some African societies where from time to time there was a male shortage, the culture felt very strongly that every woman had the right to marriage and childbirth.

In the African American community, we too have a male shortage, with some cities possessing a ratio of three females to one male. Yet because of our religious and political beliefs, polygamy is outlawed but serial marriages, "shacking," and out-of-wedlock conceptions have reached epidemic proportions. What is the difference between one man being married to two women with children and being financially and spiritually responsible for both families, and one man who will be married twice and be financially and spiritually responsible for both families?

In the first scenario, both families were cared for indefinitely. Often in serial marriages, the first family becomes neglected by the man when he enters into a second marriage. We won't even discuss the qualitative loss of shacking and out-of-wedlock conception where often the woman is financially and spiritually responsible for the family. I believe one of the major reasons why we keep entering relationships, despite the horrifying statistics, is because the Lord made us *needy*.

In the first seven days when the Lord made the heaven and earth, divided darkness from light, made herbs, grass, sun, moon, stars, and animals, each day the Lord said that it was good. But when the Lord made man, Scripture says the Lord said it is not good that man should live alone. **The Lord made us needy.** The Lord made us complementary to each other. He saw that man was unhappy by himself. Out of man He would provide his complement and from that date to this they would have a "need" for each other.

The problem is that we have superseded our relationship with each other over God. Many people now feel that if they are not in a relationship they are not happy. Many of us have never been taught that we need to first have a relationship with the Lord, and that there is a parallel between our relationship with God and our relationship with each other. The closer our relationship with God, the closer our relationship will be with our mate. By contrast, a poor relationship with God will lead to a poor relationship with another.

Elizabeth Achtemeier in the book *The Committed Marriage*, says:

> Human beings are first of all creatures of a sovereign Creator who are made to live an ongoing and loving relationship with the God who has made them. Any definition of human life that leaves out that divine human relationship is automatically going to be incomplete or distorted. In fact, affirms the Biblical faith, the health and outcome of human life are basically determined by that relationship, and the preservation of the wholeness of the living relationship with God is thus determinative of all other facets of human living. Applied to marriage, then, the affirmation is that the relationship with God or the marital partners - or lack of it - will have a basic influence on their union, second in importance

to no other factor. In short, faith in God is not something added on to an otherwise healthy or unhealthy
marriage. It affects, often decisively, every facet of
the union.[3]

Many people think they can apply mathemati-
cal rules in the classroom to mathematical rules in God's
creation. We were taught in school that one half plus
one half equals one. In relationships, one half plus
one half does not equal one. One half and one half
equals a marriage that is incomplete. In God's math
one plus one equals one. The same is true in the African value system MAAT.

People often bring their deficiencies to the relationships and believe they can be overcome by their
mates. Many unhappy people look for happiness with
and in their mates. People that suffer from low self-
esteem believe that the addition of another person
will make them complete. This is also illustrated when
people buy clothes, cars and houses thinking "things"
will make them happy. People that are incomplete,
who are less than whole, are always looking for someone else to make them complete.

Everyone longs to give themselves completely
to someone. To have a deep soulful relationship
with another. To be loved thoroughly and exclusively. God says no. Not until you are satisfied,
fulfilled and content with living and being loved by
Me alone, with giving yourself totally or unreserv-
edly with Me alone.
I am God and I am your source, not your spouse. I
love you my child and until you discover that only in
Me is your satisfaction to be found, you will not be
capable to enjoy the perfect human relationship that

45

I have planned for you. You will never be united with another until you are first united with Me. Exclusive of anyone or anything else, exclusive of any other desires and longings, I want you to stop planning, stop wishing and allow Me to give you the most thrilling plan that you can't imagine. I want you to have the very best. Please allow Me to bring it to you.

Just keep your eyes on Me, expecting the greatest things to be done. Keep learning and listening to the things I tell you. You must be patient and wait. Don't be anxious . . . don't worry . . . don't look around at things others have gotten or that I've given to them. Don't look at the things you think you want, just keep looking to Me. Or you will miss what I want to give you and then when you are ready, I will surprise you with a love far more wonderful than you can ever dream.

You see until you are ready and until the one I have for you is ready, I am working even this very minute to have both of you with me in the life I have prepared for you. You won't be able to experience the love that exemplifies your relationship with Me and this is perfect love. And dear one, I want you to have this most wonderful love. I want you to see in the flesh a picture of your relationship with Me and to enjoy materially and concretely the everlasting union of beauty and perfection. I am God Almighty, believe and be satisfied.[4]

An illustration of an incomplete relationship and/or marriage is when you have one partner acting like the parent and the other like the child. This is a *parasitic* relationship because the parent needs a mate to control and the child needs a mate to take care of him or her.

A parent-child relationship is not ideal and often leads to emotional and physical abuse. In most cases, the child seeks to become an adult and the parent's low self-esteem and obsession to control is unable to remain in a relationship with an empowered adult. Marriage can only be successful with two adults, but not a parent and child.

Many brothers in relationships, themselves victims of sexism, learn and then brag in the bars, barber shops and the locker rooms that you have to "break her down" and then "rebuild" her to your specifications. You would think they were talking about a car and not one of God's children.

Many times when I'm on talk shows talking about the science of selecting a mate, invariably there will be men and women calling in stating that they are a good person, and wondering why they can't find a good mate. This question has challenged me tremendously, especially when asked by good men, because so many women tell me there are very few good men still available. Yet these good men consistently call in and tell me that they can't find good women. I ponder why this good man has not met any of the last 10-15 good women who were our previous callers.

Do you think maybe the reason why good men end up with bad women and vice versa is because we place too much emphasis on external beauty? Many times good brothers try to convince me that they can't find good women after making the object of their desires the finest women based on European standards.

Many brothers who tell me how good they are, when I ask them where they were looking for their mate, or where did they find this bad woman that they are now with, they indicate that it was at the bar, party, or in the store. Many of these good people have a problem because they are looking for someone outside of themselves to make them happy.

Often people that define themselves as good ironically suffer from low self-esteem at the gut level and don't feel worthy of being with a good person. Many people also choose mates that need them. Their self-esteem is so low that it is only boosted by being around dependent people.

In addition, some of these "good" people allow themselves to be attracted to opposites. They define themselves as good because they're very studious, but rather than valuing their level of scholarship, they choose a party animal.

Frequently, these people also feel they can change or convert the other person. This classic malady some African American women suffer from by ignoring obvious problems while believing they can play God and convert their mate. Sometimes good people tell me they are simply naive and gullible, and the people they thought were positive, were dishonest and manipulative. Lastly, some of these good people may not be as good as they thought they were. It's a self-evaluation and you have to wonder what criteria they were using. Some people define themselves as good based solely upon looks, income, and degrees.

In this first stage of a relationship, which is sometimes called courting or looking for the evidence, we should not solely rely on our own observation. I was watching a talk show and a 16-year-old girl told her mother on national television that she wanted to get married today. In spite of her mother's objections she proceeded accordingly. In traditional Africa, people could not marry without the permission of their parents and elders. To assure a complementary union, elders from both families talked with each other and shared their child's weaknesses, strengths, needs and desires.

I just don't believe that a young person or older person can make the correct decision while falling in love. Personally, I don't believe that anyone should make a decision while falling, and I also believe that collective decisions are more effective. I'm also concerned about pastors and churches that will marry people without any premarital counseling or, at best, one or two sessions and often conducted by inexperienced, unmarried counselors.

I was pleased in talking with some pastors to hear them say two things are operative before they marry someone in their church. The first is a 40-hour session over a period of four to eight weeks. Second is that only *after* successful completion of the premarital counseling will the church then decide whether they will marry the couple. Too often couples are allowed to set the date and plan the wedding while receiving their last few minutes of counseling which falls the day before the wedding. When premarital counseling is designed in that way, it is obvious that it is not being taken seriously by either party. The whole objective of premarital counseling is to assess whether this couple is ready to make one of the most important decisions of their lives.

I'm frequently looking for research projects. Two excellent studies would be the nature and impact of premarital counseling on marital stability. Another would be the location of the wedding and its impact on marital stability.

The three most popular places for weddings are the church, the judge's chambers and some secular cultural location. There is a strong possibility that if you see the judge on the front end there's a very good chance you will see the judge on the back end. If you see the judge in your wedding, you probably will see the judge at your divorce. If you are married in a secular cultural location where the talk show rappers, soap opera, barber, beauty shop and locker room and bar experts gravitate, there's a very good chance your divorce will be discussed in that same setting. I believe that the divorce rate is lower if you are married in a church. The divorce rate can also be high in church if the pre-marital counseling was lacking and if they were in church and not in *Christ*.

A recent study indicated that 75 percent of all marriages are held in the church, yet only 40 percent of Americans attend church. Fewer still read the Scriptures, pray and confess that Jesus Christ is Lord.[5] In my church, we had to alter the policy on who was eligible to get married in church because there were people who were joining on one Sunday and booking a wedding reservation for the church the following Sunday. Many of those people, I never saw again.

I remember that on our wedding day in the church, hundreds of people, a big reception and a honeymoon to some luxurious island awaited us. Often when you're reciting your vows you really don't know what you're saying. Rita and I have often laughed at the fact that during those moments you will almost say anything. The pastor could be speaking another language, but you really don't understand and internalize all of its significance. Often pastors will say when the crowds have left, when the reception is over and the honeymoon is concluded, play the wedding vows back and repeat them again. Each anniversary Rita and I have done that and the vows become more meaningful every time we hear them. We try to visualize who those people were years ago that made those promises. Did they really know what they were doing, but more importantly, who they were making those vows to?

We now move to the second stage of the relationship and that's the *romantic stage*. This is the feel-good stage, the stage where you can run through grassy fields in slow motion with your spouse and your feet never touch the ground. It is a stage where all that's required of you is to feel good. It's the stage where you offer your first and best impression.

It is similar to the first "high," and unfortunately, many of us will spend the rest of our lives trying to recapture that first experience, that first kiss, that first hug. The first date, as when the addict is trying to replicate the first high. It is the stage where there is no history; you just met one another; everything is new; everything you learn about the person is new and exciting. What makes the romantic stage so exhilarating is that everything is new and we have a culture that is based on change, and narcissism.

The romantic stage becomes for many the stage of ecstasy. It is the stage that is sung about so well by Smokey Robinson, Luther Vandross, Anita Baker, and Sade. My wife says that in these beautiful love songs that mesmerize us, the singers lie so well. They're so convincing, but the words are so unrealistic.

I was trying to find a love song that would reflect how naive we are to think that love can last forever. How can two people actually promise they will stay in love with each other forever. Ironically the song that O.J. Simpson and Nicole Brown played on their wedding day, sung by the Four Tops, "I Believe in You and Me," illustrates why it is so difficult to remain there forever. Read the words carefully.

I believe in you and me.
I believe that we will be in love eternally.
As far as I can see,
You will always be the one for me.
Oh yes you will.
I believe in dreams again,
I believe that love will never end.
And like the river finds the sea,
I was lost, now I'm free.

I believe in you and me.
I will never leave your side,
I will never hurt your pride.
When all the chips are down,
I will always be around.
Just to be right where you are.
My love, oh I love you girl.
I will never leave you out.
I will always let you in.
To places no one's ever been.
Can't you see?
I believe in you and me.
Maybe I'm a fool, to feel the way I do.
But I would play the fool forever,
Just to be with you forever.
I believe in miracles, love is a miracle.

And baby you're a dream come true.
I was lost.
Now I'm free girl.
I believe in you and me.[6]

The most frequently used words are *love, always, never,* and *forever.* O.J. and Nicole naively thought that this song was expressing their love. In most cases it's not humanly possible for a person to say that I will *never* leave you. I will *always* be there. Our love is *forever.* This love can only come from God. Think of all the people in your life who said they would always love you, that it was forever, and they would never leave you. Where are they now? The best man can do is *try* to be like God.

As much as I love Smokey Robinson's music, his songs "Ooo Baby," "Baby I'll Try Something New," "Baby Come Close" and all of his other brilliant songs were unable to save his marriage. Let's juxtapose the Four Tops' "I Believe in You and Me" with the gospel song sung by Vicki Winans, "Like No Other Love" and then we will better understand the difference between secular and agape love.

> The way that you love me
> Nobody else can
> What's the use of this life
> If there's no one to share it with?
> And all the pain of this life is easier,
> with someone to bear it with
> That special day that we met.
> The one I won't soon forget.
> Your love has proved to me.
> It has never failed me yet.

And the way that you love me.
Shows when you hold me.
Whenever I'm lonely,
you're always there.
The way you embrace me
No other can.
The way that you love me,
like no other man.
I've come to know sweeter days,
as I spend my time with you.
I found there is no better way.
That's why I tell the whole wide world of you.
Of the day that we met.
The one I won't soon forget.
Your love was good to me.
It has never failed me yet.

And the way that you love me
shows when you hold me, hold me, hold me.
Whenever I'm lonely,
you're always there.
I didn't know when we met.
It was the day I won't forget.
Your love has proved to me.
It has never failed me yet.

The way you embrace me,
nobody else can
The way that you love me,
is like no other man.[7]

Can you imagine all this time we have been expecting someone to love us like the Lord? Only God can use the words *always*, *never*, and *forever*. Humans can try, but only the Lord can succeed.

Renita Weems, the brilliant religious scholar and writer, says secular love is like a feeling, it comes and goes.[8] Professor Robert Staples says love lasts about 15 months.[9] Many people say, "I love you because you make me feel good." That is not love, it's self-gratification. Many of us simply have unrealistic expectations in the romantic stage. We're trying to replace a love that we've never known from the Lord with a love we desire in the secular world only to be extremely disappointed.

Stage three becomes the *problem* stage. The same person who can make you feel so good on Friday night is now on your last nerve Saturday morning. In *The Power, Passion and Pain of Black Love,* I mentioned the ten major problems fueling this high divorce rate in America. These problems include the lack of spirituality, low self-esteem, the lack of communication, economics, which includes either the lack of money or its mismanagement, coparenting and stepparenting, racism, drugs, sexism, infidelity or the lack of sexual compatibility and in-laws.[10]

It behooves all of us before we get married to develop a defense against the above factors. It is naive to assume that if these are some of Satan's major tools for divorce, that none of these are going to affect our relationship. When I speak to couples in the romantic stage who are considering marriage, I try to make marriage as mundane as possible because they think the romantic stage is forever. I mention diapers, dishes, homework, bills and sex possibly Tuesday at 10:30 pm. My pastor says brothers have been tricked into believing that they were going to marry

Clare Huckstable. She went to bed in a satin gown with her hair looking beautiful and awoke the next morning with no wrinkles in the satin gown and her hair was still beautiful without curlers. He reminds us that marriage is cotton pajamas, plaid socks, rollers, a discolored scarf around the head, Vicks vapor rub on the chest, Noxzema on the face and "passing gas" in the bed!

I just want to add, brothers don't look like Denzel Washington when they wake up. Many of us wear faded pajamas, have stinky breath, snore, whatever hair is left is uncombed and we also pass gas. We often spend more time with the fellas, our business, the liberation struggle or time in the church. We do less housework than our wives, while leaving clothes and shoes everywhere. We complain about our wife's weight, while developing a pot and beer belly that is leaning over the belt buckle.

I believe we need a realistic view of marriage. Renita Weems says, "Marriage is more than you imagined, but less than you fantisized."[11] Marriage is an empty box. People are expected to do something for marriage. If you do not put into the box more than you take out, it becomes empty. Many of us spend our entire lives vacillating between the romantic and problem stages. We never realize the problems may be with us and not with our mates. We think changing mates will change our circumstance. Renita Weems reminds us that many of us have not made a commitment to God, but made a commitment to *better*. We made a commitment to a better face, better body, better legs, better money, better clothes, and better houses. And if that's the case, then we will always seek someone better across the street.

This concept was made personal for me because being a world traveler, I have seen some of the finest African women that any brother could possibly imagine. Not only have I seen the finest women, I've seen some of the smartest and most brilliant women that any brother could fathom. I've talked with sisters on fire for the Lord. I've known women who have beautiful personalities and can provide a home and a meal that any brother would desire. If my commitment was to *better*, I would seek a new mate each week. Instead, I thank God for my wife who is the *best*.

I began to look for Biblical role models who possessed similar challenges. I studied the life of David and Solomon. Steve Farrar mentioned in the book *Point Man* that many of us reach a midlife crisis. We believe marriage becomes easier after five years, but then you experience the seven-year itch. Others postulate that after ten years the marriage becomes stable. Satan tries to deceive us to relax and take off our whole armor. In order to have a successful marriage you have to work at it each and every day. Unfortunately, David and Solomon had a midlife crisis. David, who had a heart like God, made a critical mistake with Bathsheba. Solomon, who was very wise, made a grave mistake and married over 300 women and began to worship their gods. Many men run 95 meters in a 100-meter race. It appeared that everything was going well. They had a good job, house, and car, possessed a beautiful wife and children, but were unable to complete the race.

It becomes even more challenging to exit the problem stage when there's an acute male shortage with a two:one female to male ratio. While women have been socialized to respond favorably or unfavorably depending upon who's asking, many men have not been taught. Many men who have played the hunter lack the experience to respond to the new women who "hit" on the brothers. Some men feel their masculinity is threatened if they don't respond. The midlife crisis that many men are experiencing is not exclusively reserved for men. While 75 percent of men are involved in extramarital affairs, 50 percent of women are.[12] The problem stage is further complicated for African American women when their man suffers from the O.J. Simpson disease and leaves them for a White woman. If anyone is going to leave the race it would be the group with the shortage. The reality is there's a three to one ratio of men to women that are marrying outside the race.[13]

Due to the shortage of African American men, African American women are now increasing in aggregate numbers in relation to becoming more involved with White men. I used to believe interracial relationships were the greatest irritant to African American women until sisters began sharing with me that they're losing more men to homosexuality. This has now become further complicated when some men choose a life of bisexuality. What is an African American woman to do when her husband says I want to stay with you, but I also want to be with him?

The obstacles and land mines in the first three stages prevent most of us from ever reaching the *commitment* stage. This is the stage where you and your mate realize that regardless of who you're with, there will be problems, so I might as well stay in the relationship and work them out.

My wife says marriage is what you make it. Marriage requires work and unfortunately in the secular songs we have not been taught to work. We must continue to date each other throughout the marriage. I've spoken to many couples who have allowed children and work to prevent them from romancing each other. We work harder at our careers, jobs, and hobbies than our marriages.

Many marriages have grown stale and exist in name only. Optimal marriages require work, dating and a quick resolution of conflict. Ideally, couples try never going to bed angry. I have spoken to people that were on their deathbeds who were highly respected in their field, but I've never heard one of them say they wish they could have attended one more meeting, spoken in one more seminar, or completed one more business acquisition. They all invariably regret they had not spent more time with their family.

I believe it is virtually impossible to reach stage four without a personal relationship with the Lord. In her book *The Committed Marriage*, Elizabeth Achtemeir makes a parallel between your love for the Lord and your spouse. This profound prayer reads as follows:

> That I may come nearer to her, draw me nearer to Thee then to her. That I may know her, make me know Thee more than her. That I may love her with the perfect love of a perfectly whole heart, cause me to love Thee more than her and most of all, that nothing may be between me and her, be Thou between us, every moment. That we may be constantly together, draw us into separate loneliness with Thyself. And when we meet breast to breast, oh God let it be upon thine own.[14]

Scripture teaches that ye are bone of my bone and flesh of my flesh. Howard Hewett, in one of his beautiful love songs, "For the Lover in You," says when a man provides a house, she will provide him with a home. When he provides her with food, she'll provide him with a meal. When he gives her his seed, she'll give him their baby. Oba T'Shaka, in *The Mother Principle,* describes the Maatian balance between man and woman. He is a producer and she is a creator.

In a Godly relationship there is little tension with the man being head of the house. This reverent position requires him to be the spiritual leader and to love her the way Christ loved the church and as he loved his own body. I have yet to meet a woman who would not feel comfortable with a man being the head of the house, if she knew that he would never make a decision, if he did not first submit to God and seek her opinion.

Love and commitment are prerequisites for marriage. Love is giving, forgiving and is unconditional. Commitment is mature and realizes problems exist in any marriage. Therefore rather than escaping into a fantasy relationship, sometimes called an affair, the person stays in the marriage and *works* through the problems.

The book of Malachi said the Lord hates divorce. Seldom do you ever see in the Scriptures the word *hate* next to the Lord. The good news is if you pray together daily and are obedient He will pour you out a blessing that transcends all understanding. Now that we have the marriage issue resolved, we are prepared for the next chapter, on fatherhood.

CHAPTER FOUR

FATHERHOOD

King David was deeply moved, and went up to the chamber over the gate, and wept. And as he wept, he said thus: Oh my son Absalom - my son, my son - Absalom - if only I had died in your place. O Absalom, my son, my son. 2 Samuel 18:33. *Good News Translation*

So he got up and started back to his father. He was still a long way from home when his father saw him; his heart was filled with pity, and he ran, threw his arms around his son, and kissed him.
Luke 15:20. *Good News Translation*

Satan knows that the best way to destroy the family is to separate the father from the family. White America also knows the best way to destroy the Black family is to deny the African American man the opportunity to work. One of Satan's most successful tricks is divide and conquer. I'd like to dedicate this chapter to my father, Eddie Brown. In my biased opinion, he is one of the best fathers any son could possibly have. I have one of the most dependable fathers in the world and my name Jawanza means dependable.

I have a father who worked the evening shift at the post office from 3:00 p.m. to 11:00 p.m., and while he made breakfast for my sister and me every morning, he called us at 8:00 p.m. every night throughout my childhood. If he promised he was going to attend my track meet, concert, debate or any other activity that I was involved in, he was always there. There were times when I would have a track meet at 5:00 p.m. and he would take off work for an hour. I always knew I could turn around before I approached the starting line and know he was present. Can you imagine the confidence children possess knowing they can depend on their father?

Unfortunately, almost 70 percent of African American fathers don't physically live with their children, much less give moral guidance and nurturance. In our society fatherhood is becoming more nebulous and difficult to define. We live in a culture where people try to replace fathers with sperm banks, and the state becomes the provider and the protector.

In the excellent book by David Blankenhorn, *Fatherless America*, he gives a definition for fathers:

> In a larger sense, the fatherhood story is the irreplaceable basis of culture's most urgent imperative: the socialization of males. More than any other culture invention, fatherhood guides men away from violence by fastening their behavior to a fundamental social purpose. By enjoining men to care for their children and for the mothers of their children, the fatherhood story is society's most important contrivance for shaping male identity. For men, marriage is the precondition, the enabling context, for fatherhood as a social role. Why? Because marriage fosters paternal certainty, thus permitting the emergence of what anthropologists called the legitimacy principle. This is my child, not another man's child. In turn, paternal certainty permits and encourages paternal investment: the commitment of the father

to the well-being of the child. By contrast, in "mere nature where there are no matrimonial laws," males simply impregnate females and then move on. All responsibility for children is on the mother. Paternity is absent in the state of nature. Fatherhood is a defining characteristic of a civil society. "The emergence of fatherhood as a social role for men signifies the transition from barbarism to society."[1]

Tragically we are now beginning to see signs of a society returning to barbarism. A country where humans are now beginning to act like animals of a lower species. We are now witnessing a fatherless America. We are now a culture where fathers do not exist; where their roles have become unclear and institutions have attempted to fill their void. If you need a baby, contact the sperm bank. If you need economic assistance, we can provide welfare or employment. If you need protection, we can provide car and house alarms, self-defense courses and gadgets, and handguns.

We used to live in a culture where men were the spiritual leaders in their homes. These were African men that devoured the Word, led Bible study in their homes and led the family in prayer. They were actively involved in the church's growth and development. These spiritual leaders took pride in the responsibility given in Ephesians 5 of being the head of the house and secured only by having a personal relationship with the Lord.

Steve Farrar, in his book *Point Man,* asked more than 1,000 Christian men across the United States how often in a typical week they read the Bible. Forty-five percent reported one time a week or less. The majority of these men are committed Christians and attend church more than once a week. They are not on the fringes of the church. Most would be considered pillars of their local congregations. Yet nearly half of them are spiritually illiterate and powerless.[2]

In my book, *Adam! Where Are You? Why Most Black Men Don't Go to Church*, most churches possess a 75 percent female and 25 percent male population.[3] Large numbers of African American men are staying away from the church. As long as African American men stay away from God, the African American family will remain impotent.

White America is also becoming more and more concerned about fatherless America now with 25 percent of their children living in households where the father is absent. It has been said that when White America catches a cold, Black America catches the flu; this saying is so aptly expressed in our 66 percent figure of children reared in single-parent homes. The African American family has never reached this level of single parenting. I mentioned in the "First Generation" chapter that this trend is likely to increase unless there is a serious response from the African American community to return fathers to the home.

The same chapter says that due to the concentration of poverty, we now have housing developments where 93 percent of the households consist of single parents. We have housing developments where there may not be one African American male in the entire complex. Unfortunately, we have sons who have never seen their fathers, never seen a Black man work, read, pray, or respect a woman.

One of the major reasons why African American boys are unable to reconcile their differences with each other is because they have never seen an African American man say he is sorry and reconcile his differences through non-violence. One of the earlier definitions that we gave for fatherhood describes the tremendous importance a father's role plays in the socialization of his children, especially his male children. The consequence of fathers who are not visible and actively involved in raising their sons is best described by Blankenhorn:

> There are exceptions of course, but here is the rule: Boys raised by traditionally masculine fathers generally do not commit crimes. Fatherless boys commit crimes. Both clinical studies and anthropological investigations confirm the process through which boys seek to separate from their mothers in search of the meaning of their maleness.[4]

In this process, the father is irreplaceable. He enables the son to separate from the mother. He is the gatekeeper guiding his son into the community of men, teaching him to name the meaning of his embodiment, showing him on good authority that he can be man enough. In this process, the boy becomes more than a son of his mother, or even a son of his parents. He becomes the son of his father. Later when the boy becomes a man, he will reunite with the world of women, the world of his mother, through his spouse and children. In this sense, only by becoming his father's as well as his mother's son can he become a good father and husband.

When this process of male identity does not succeed - when the boy cannot separate from the mother and become the son of his father - clinical rage results. Rage against the mother, against women, against society. It is a deeply misogynistic rage vividly expressed in contemporary rap music with titles such as "Beat That Bitch with a Bat."

Our boys live in a world totally controlled by women. They live in households where their mother, grandmother or older sister tells them what to do. They attend schools where female teachers and principals become their authority figures. Boys need quality men who can give them a sense of direction. Unfortunately, the most visible and available males seem to be gang members and/or drug dealers, both having done a terrible job in the socialization of our children.

I don't want to paint a dismal picture, but the reality is that 66 percent of our boys are going to be raised only by mothers. However, I do believe that women can effectively raise their boys, and in the next chapter, on motherhood, I offer some successful techniques for raising sons.

When we look at the different parenting styles between fathers and mothers, I am reminded of the Old and New Testaments and the concept of justice versus mercy. Generally, fathers believe in raising their children according to the law and justice. While most mothers believe in grace and mercy for their children, especially their sons, to whom they give options. If mothers give their sons options on whether they will attend afterschool and Saturday cultural awareness, tutorial, test taking, rites of passage and other enrichment activities, or stay at home, sleep, watch television, play basketball and eat pizza, which will they choose?

Generally, fathers tend to be less tolerant with their sons staying at home indefinitely. Most fathers are much more conservative with money and are less willing to buy their sons designer gym shoes and starter jackets. During my own childhood if I wanted more money I could get it from my mother, while my father not only was frugal with the money, but always wanted to give me his war stories, long walks to school and working 16 hours a day in factories and how difficult it was to earn a dollar bill.

Some fathers believe high expectations are more significant than mother's unconditional love. I will never forget my father's criticism of my performance in a championship track meet. I placed second and my father felt I should have won. I wanted him to appreciate my performance based on all the people that I beat versus the one person who beat me. My mother, on the other hand, took my side and praised me for a second-place finish. Even to this day, my father says, "I could have won that race."

One style of parenting is not better than the other. They both have value and both are needed. The ideal parent relationship is complementary and harmonious. Children raised in households where only law and justice rules have hard hearts and lack forgiveness. Children raised in households exclusively with "grace and mercy" become irresponsible.

There is an inverse relationship between fathers in the home and crime in the neighborhood. Unfortunately, if there's an absence of fathers, crime increases. We have too many boys with guns primarily because we have too few fathers in the home. Crime increases in neighborhoods without fathers because neighborhoods without men able and willing to confront youth, chase threatening gangs and reproach delinquent fathers are at risk. The absence of fathers deprives the communities of those little platoons that informally, but often effectively, control boys on the street.

The U.S. Department of Justice provides the most comprehensive source of national data on violent crimes against women. One survey's findings confirms the thesis that violent behavior among men is strongly linked to marital status. For example, about 57,000 women per year were violently assaulted by their husbands. By contrast, 200,000 women per year were assaulted by boyfriends, and 216,000 by ex-husbands. Of all the violent crimes against women committed by intimates during this period, about 65 percent were committed by either boyfriends or ex-husbands, compared with 9 percent by husbands.[5]

While there is a wealth of research illustrating the need for sons to have fathers, it is equally important for girls. The consequence of boys growing up without fathers is they will turn to guns while girls without fathers will turn to having babies. There are African American girls who have never been hugged in a nonsexual way by a man. They have been played with by boys 15 to 25 years of age, but they have never been hugged by their father. Unfortunately, some girls who have not been hugged by their father begin to turn toward other men for that kind of nurturance. This kind of affection - daddy's love - can't be replaced by mothers, who have often done everything humanly possible for their daughters.

In the following chapter, we'll discuss young girls who are caught by older males with weak raps. These are boys masquerading as surrogate fathers.

From a quantitative perspective, the consequence of girls growing up without fathers is that daughters of single parents are 53 percent more likely to marry as teenagers, 111 percent more likely to have children as teenagers, 164 percent more likely to have a premarital birth and 92 percent more likely to dissolve their own marriages.[6]

Why is it so difficult for African American men to be fathers? Listed on the following page are social categories. Which group, African American women or African American men, suffer greater in these areas?

Which Group Suffers the Most? You decide.

	African American Men	or	African American Women
Infant mortality			
Remedial reading classes			
Special education placement			
Suspension			
High school dropout			
College dropout			
Gang involvement			
Criminal activity			
Alcohol and nicotine consumption			
Consumption of heroin and cocaine			
Incarceration			
Mental institutions			
Homeless			
Homicide			
Suicide			
Lower life expectancy			

These factors contribute to the sparse participation of African American males in their families. If we as a people are going to reduce and eradicate the problems in the African American family, we're going to have to address these factors. In the introduction, I said the

70

Fatherhood

two greatest problems facing the African American family were lack of a relationship with God and unemployment.

In 1920, 90 percent of Black youth had their fathers at home. In 1960, it was 80 percent, but in 2002 it had declined to only 32 percent. This can be paralleled with the change in the economy from agriculture to manufacturing to information technology, services and retail trade. Robert Staples points out that the unemployment rate for African American males is three times that of White males.[7] We have been taught to believe that the change in the economy is race and gender neutral. White supremacy affects everything, including unemployment rates. When manufacturing jobs close, African American males are the first to be terminated and the last to be hired in the service sector.

I have a good friend, a hardworking African American woman working two jobs, who takes the position that in spite of the change in the economy, work is available for the African American man, and if she can find two jobs, surely he can find one. While I think her analysis is simplistic within the context of the global economy and monopoly capitalism, I continue to contemplate her perspective. I would not advocate we could employ all African American men with a simple statement that work is available.

Just as I remind African American women that they don't need to be overwhelmed by the 2:1 ratio of the male shortage because all they need is one man. The same applies with African American men who read about the 25 percent male unemployment rate, because all they need is one job. I acknowledged to my

71

friend that there are taxis to be driven, cars to be washed, appliances to be repaired, lawn work to be done, and dishes to be washed.

I believe if you can sell, you will never be unemployed. You can volunteer for a company and if they like your workstyle, you can create your own job from that experience. When I was 14, I volunteered with a company. They gave me bus money the first week, spending money the second week, and during the fifth week when somebody quit, they hired me for the position.

My friend reminds me of a story of a couple who had five children. They both worked. She was a school teacher and he worked in a factory. They returned home one evening after work and he told her he had quit, because his manhood and pride had been violated.

When it was time for dinner, she placed seven empty plates on the table and told her children, "your father quit his job because his pride was violated and so tonight, we will eat his pride." The next day and for several months, while he moped around the house, she, college degreed, did domestic work after teaching school. She believed, like my friend, that work is available, children need to eat, and all work is honorable.

In the chapter on the village, I will describe two macroeconomic programs that I believe can stimulate the Black economy. We cannot allow Ford, GM, Chrysler, IBM, and Xerox to define our masculinity. The Lord, not the Fortune 500, made us and we cannot allow the Fortune 500 and the Trilateral Commission to break our spirit. We cannot allow the Fortune 500 to separate us from our families and reduce us from fathers, husbands, and men to sperm donors, shackers, and boys who no longer feel worthy to stay with their families.

72

The disease of fatherlessness in our families is not only creating social, psychological, and moral problems, but it's also creating financial hardships. The loaded term "feminization of poverty" assumes that African American males are doing relatively well when that obviously is not true. It also mitigates the reality that White women are also doing better financially than African American men. In spite of this clarification, women, both White and Black are experiencing financial hardships without their husbands in the home.

In married homes in the United States in 2002, about 13 percent of all children under the age of six lived in poverty. In single-mother families, about 66 percent of young children lived in poverty. In married homes with preschool children, the median family income in 2002 was approximately $41,000. In single-mother homes with young children, the median income was about $9,000. Of all married families in the nation in 2002, about 6 percent lived in poverty. Of all the female-headed families, about 35 percent lived in poverty. Of all the Black married couples with children under the age of 18 in 2002, about 15 percent lived in poverty. Of all the Black-single-mother-headed homes with children, about 57 percent lived in poverty.[8]

How can a truck driver make $12 an hour and a secretary make $6? How can a custodial engineer make $30,000 and a classroom teacher make $25,000? This is an example of sexism and the feminization of poverty.

The government now feels they can replace fathers with mandatory child support payments. The concept proposes that the male income is more significant than the male presence. Child support enforcement has become a major industry for the government with a bureaucracy employing as of 2002 about 230 federal officials and 38,000 state officials.[9]

The complexity of the child support industry is that there are different types of fathers that are involved with our children. We have absent fathers, sperm donors, significant others, stepfathers, visiting fathers, deadbeat dads, and real fathers. When the government becomes involved with this issue of trying to enforce child support payments, many times they are looking for people who have never declared, acknowledged, recognized nor identified as being the father.

Absent Fathers

We now live in a culture where two consenting adults are involved in sex, but the father has never accepted the reality of being the father nor has the mother held him accountable. They do not think of themselves as deadbeat dads precisely because they do not think of themselves as dads. These men never signed anything. They never agreed to play by any fatherhood code. They have never had any explicit obligations to either their children or to the mother of their children.

Moreover, the mother increasingly affirm this same view of fatherhood, probably because they don't want these guys around. When asked by the Census Bureau why they receive no child support payments, never-married mothers are more likely than married mothers to say they did not pursue an award or did not want an award. For these mothers, the father did not leave. He was never there in the first place. As a result, he is not a likely source for child support payments, nor is he a likely candidate for fatherhood.

I receive numerous letters from fathers around the country who want to spend more time with their children. Their concern is with the state and their ex-spouses treating them as a money source without providing them with the opportunity to have visitation privileges. For example, according to the Census Bureau data, about 78 percent of all absent fathers in 2000 who had visitation privileges with their children, were also obligated to specific child support payment schedules. Again more visits, more payments.

Yet while 67 percent of all divorce fathers had visitation privileges in 2002, only 33 percent of all the new style absent fathers, those who had never married the mother, had visitation privileges. Another study continues to reinforce this by saying that among absent fathers, those whose children were born outside of marriage are less involved with their children on all dimensions, paying support, visiting, and decision making, than those whose children were born in marriage.[10]

It is unfortunate that fathers are viewed purely from their economic resources and not the full dimensions of their character. You can't compare a $30,000 dad to a $3,000 child support check. The dad provides income, protection, nurturance and spiritual direction. His $30,000 is used to pay expenses throughout the house including mortgage, utilities, cars, appliances, food, etc. If he leaves, the family will suffer a net loss of $27,000 in addition to what real men provide for their families. Unfortunately, when many fathers physically leave the home, not only do they not provide financial resources, but they also do not allocate the time and emotional nurturance children need.

I hear heartbreaking stories about fathers who promised they would pick the child up at 2:00 p.m. on Saturday and mothers having to watch their children cry into the evening because he never arrived. What is involved in the psyche of African American men who do this to their children? Do divorce, unemployment and affairs exempt men from fatherhood?

Ironically, some men after divorcing one wife enter a new relationship with another woman who has children. He provides economic and moral resources for his new home, but ignores his biological children. Not only do we need to look at the psyche of the African American man that is involved with this dynamic, but equally significant is the African American woman who, rather than encouraging her new husband to be responsible toward his biological children encourages him to ignore them. Doesn't she realize that if he could do that to his first family, it could very well happen to her?

Children should not lose their daddies because their parents divorced. Many children believe they cause the breakup. Children deserve minimally a periodic call, visit and birthday and holiday gift.

Sperm Donors

I mentioned at the outset of this chapter that as our society becomes more and more fatherless, not only the actual numbers but the value of fatherhood is diminished. For example, on the talk show circuit you'll see famous single African American females who desire a child, but not a husband and father. Many women knew it was a one-night stand. Other women sought out a particular man because of his genetic possibilities. Women are also going to the sperm bank for artificial insemination. Sperm donors are increasing in our society.

Significant Other

The concept of fatherhood has been replaced by some with the term "significant other." We no longer expect fathers to be in attendance for school luncheons and other activities. What are schools to do about father activities with only 34 percent of our children having their fathers at home? They were forced to call it "significant other day" in deference to the 66 percent majority without fathers. I mentioned in the "First Generation" chapter a father who had three boys in the kindergarten class, by three different mothers. I don't think schools had this kind of father in mind when they wanted to recognize fathers.

The significant other concept becomes more confusing to children because so many men have served in that role. Children wonder how many significant others their mother will have. Boys resent these men because they usurp their own roles as "man of the house." Girls are also watching their mothers and they quickly learn women don't need men, husbands or fathers, they simply need a male. Terry McMillan told Oprah Winfrey, sometimes you just need a man for "maintenance."

Stepfather

The next type of father is the stepparent. His numbers have been increasing over the past two decades by an astonishing 40 percent. There are an estimated six million stepfathers now living in America. Less than 15 percent of the entire American population will live with the same father for 18 years of their lives.[11]

My concern about the prefix "step" is based on the European concept of hierarchal relationships. How can a man who was only there for two or three minutes, who only provided sperm, be called father? And the one who stayed for years, paid the bills, protected and nurtured be called stepfather? Fatherhood is more sociological than biological.

There are tremendous challenges to being a step-father. In blended families, there are countless scenarios based on the involvement of the ex-spouses, age, gender, personality, and number of children. Stepparenting an infant girl whose biological father is absent is far different than stepparenting four teen-age males whose father is present. Research shows that both stepfathers and stepmothers take a considerably less active role in parenting than do custodial parents. Even after two years, disengagement by the stepparent is the most common parental style.[12]

The challenge of blended families is also the number one reason for divorce the second time around. When we do it God's way, marriage precedes sex and children arrive after marriage, there is no divorce and stepparenting is eliminated. But when we violate God's law, we are faced with blended family challenges. But they too can be overcome within a God-fearing household.

Visiting Fathers

The next father we want to briefly explore is the visiting father, or "ice cream daddy." These are the fathers who will have their children waiting for them in the window and when they finally pick them up, they take them anywhere and everywhere with ice cream being the last stop before returning them to their mother. She then has to make sure the children eat their green vegetables and complete their chores and homework.

The "ice cream daddy" is not the ideal parent. His approach helps neither the parent nor the child. Parenting is not an every other weekend activity. Children need more than four days a month. Visiting fathers suffer from the desire to be liked, and that's why ice cream ranks higher than spinach and the playground wins over chores.

Deadbeat Dad

The next father is the deadbeat dad. This father is a drain on our society as the government tries to track him down, bring him to court, garnish wages, revoke driver's licenses and incarcerate. Many African American mothers who have never declared this person as being the father of the children have decided a welfare check is more dependable than a deadbeat dad. Many mothers would rather avoid the hassle of declaring who the father is and avoid collection procedures. They believe there is more money and less headaches drawing a welfare check than trying to track down a deadbeat dad. This is a sad commentary on fatherhood. I pray that every deadbeat dad who attended the Million Man March will resolve his financial obligations and spend time with his children. I pray that every sperm donor at the March will claim responsibility for his children.

Father

I saved the best group of fathers for last. These fathers not only stay with their children, but they stay when the mothers don't. Not all single parents are female. Three percent of African American single parents are fathers. While that's a small percentage, it is a population receiving very little media coverage. I believe if the media gave more coverage to fathers, other men would think twice before they abandoned their children. We need to promote those fathers who attend PTA meetings, Cub Scout programs, dance rehearsals and took paternity leave.

It disappoints me when professional athletes are interviewed and they only say "hi mom." I'm wondering, was it their mother who taught them how to play? Where's dad? It's inspiring to hear Tiger Woods, David Robinson, Shaq O'Neil, Grant Hill and Michael Jordan talk about their fathers. When these men are interviewed they say "hi dad and hi mom."

Boys need men to teach them rites of passage. In an agrarian economy, men took boys under their wing and taught them farming and survival skills. In this high technology economy, what is unique about the father-son relationship? When will a father have time for his children if he is no longer on the farm, but in an office eight hours a day? How many fathers take their children fishing or hunting? How many fathers show their children how to do an oil change and repair appliances? How many fathers teach their children self-defense? I pray that all fathers are teaching their children a love for the Lord, a desire for scholarship, a respect for women and economic self-sufficiency.

We need men to visit boys who impregnated a girl on the block, and is neglecting his child, to teach them to be responsible. We need men who desire to have sons; many men have told me they would prefer daughters because it's too hard to raise sons. Can you imagine, we have become so impotent that we don't want to replicate ourselves? Men need to open up and share their pain and most intimate secrets with other men and know the conversation will remain confidential. We need men who will talk about childrearing with other men.

We need men who will meet weekly and hold each other accountable on the following questions:

(1) Have you spent quality time with your wife and children this week?

(2) Have you spent daily time in prayer and in the Scriptures this week?

(3) Have you been completely above reproach in all your financial dealings this week?

(4) Have you volunteered time in your church and/ or community organization this week?

(5) Have you been with a woman other than your wife this week in a way that was inappropriate or could have looked to others as if you were using poor judgment?

(6) Have you just lied to me?

As we continue in the natural order of family development, from marriage to fatherhood, the following chapter will look at motherhood, including teen pregnancy, single-parent mothers, mothers who remain with their husbands, and grandmothers who now have to raise another generation of children.

Children need love and understanding from their fathers.

Children need love and understanding from their mothers.

CHAPTER FIVE

MOTHERHOOD

John 4: 16-18. *Jesus said to her, go call your husband and come here. The woman answered and said I have no husband. Jesus said to her, you have well said I have no husband. For you have had five husbands and the one whom you now have is not your husband. And that you spoke truly.*

Genesis 16: 11. *And the angel of the Lord said to Hagar, behold you are with child and you shall bear a son. You shall call his name Ishmael, because the Lord has heard your affliction.*

Genesis 21: 17. *And God heard the voice of the lad, then the angel of God called Hagar out of Heaven and said to her, what ails you Hagar. Fear not for God has heard the voice of the lad where he is.*

1 Kings 3: 27. *So King Solomon answered and said give the first woman the living child and by no means kill him. She is his mother.*

Proverbs 31: 28. *The children rise up and call her blessed; her husband also and he praises her.*

The New King James Translation

I dedicate this chapter to the three mothers in my life. I was blessed with a biological mother, Mary Brown, who loved me unconditionally. She also helped start my communications company by lending me $1,000. I remember how supportive she had been in all my endeavors, even when she and my father divorced and our family struggled financially.

My paternal grandmother, Cecil Prisentine, not only took care of me during my infancy when my mother was ill, but kept me almost every summer. She was the one who introduced me to Jesus. My grandmother was on fire for the Lord, and I attended Sunday school, church and returned that evening for Baptist Training Union. My parents reminded me that when my mother felt better, my grandmother was unwilling to give me back! My aunt had to intervene and remind my grandmother that I belonged to my parents. My grandmother only earned $50 a week, but when I graduated from high school, she gave me $100. I broke down and cried. When I graduated from college and was ready to assume my first full-time position, I visited my grandmother before starting. She died six months later, but I have never regretted the time I spent with my grandmother. She taught me more about Maat and the Nguzo Saba than any nationalist.

My third mother was my stepmother, Ethel Brown She was an excellent listener and became my counselor during adolescence. When my father and I were at odds concerning the direction of my life, it was my stepmother who intervened and provided the peace that my father and I needed to reconcile.

There is something special about motherhood, particularly African motherhood. African women have endured so much. They not only gave birth to the first and greatest civilization, but also had the unfortunate experience of having their children taken away from

22222222

them and into the greatest holocaust, never to be seen again. They have seen their husbands denied the respect that is due every man. They have had to endure husbands who were neither able to provide financially for their families, nor able to protect them from the onslaught of White male supremacy and the numerous rapes that took place during slavery.

In the chapter, "First Generation," I mentioned that there were two resources on which you could always count: the Lord and your mother. Before the onslaught of crack cocaine into the African American community, the bond between African mothers and their children was one that could never be broken. African motherhood is still revered, as witnessed by restaurants and entertainment centers completely full on Mother's Day. Unfortunately, on Father's Day the demand at these places is a pale comparison.

African history teaches that the African family has been "twinlineal," which is different from patriarchal, matriarchal, patrilineal, or matrilineal. The first two terms deal with power while the latter term concerns itself with lineage. Twinlineal, says Oba T'Shaka in *The Mother Principle,* describes our family systems because children are not descended solely from our mother or our father but from both.[1] The African family was rooted in agriculture and women were valued to establish a home. In transient nomadic, mobile, cultures people were constantly looking for food, and women were viewed as a liability. African men and women were in perfect balance with each other. They did not view each other from a hierarchical perspective. Only insecure people are driven to establish power relationships with each other.

In the previous chapter on fatherhood, I mentioned that the two major problems African American men are experiencing are not submitting to God and unemployment. Most African American women lament that their greatest problem is finding and keeping a godly, employed African American man. Seldom are African American men perturbed by their inability to find a mate. The African American man is primarily concerned about being able in a capitalistic, patriarchal society to provide for his family. African American women's identity is not predicated on their economic resources, but their ability to marry and give birth to children.

Due to sexism very few races and ethnic groups experience the reality that women exceed men in academic achievement and economic prosperity. In the European and Asian communities, men exceed women in educational achievement, income and wealth. In the African American, Native American and Latino American populations, the reverse is true. In 2002, there were in excess of 600,000 African American collegiate females. As the American manufacturing industry continues to erode, African American males who once earned $12 to $18 an hour in factories are forced to drive on the information super highway without reading, computer or mathematical literacy.

When I talk to women nationwide from all age groups and educational backgrounds, what I hear more than anything else is the desire to be a wife and mother. Their brilliant career is second to the desire for a family. Most women are not driven by a career and corporate America and would love to meet a man who could provide for them and their children. Very few African American women have had the wealth nor the option to stay home as possible for White women. It is insensitive and inaccurate to accuse the African American woman of being domineering when she is forced to work because her husband is absent, under-employed or unemployed.

There are numerous problems affecting the African American family, but none is more acute than the teen-age pregnancy epidemic that is not only facing America, but is literally destroying the African American family. African American females lead the world in teen pregnancy, followed by Arabs and White Americans. Incidentally, White American female teenagers would be first, but they lead the world in abortions.[2]

Many of our leaders are so concerned about rac-ism, monopoly capitalism, crime, politics, drugs, edu-cation and health care that they often overlook this teenage pregnancy epidemic. I'm no longer sure which is worse—the African American male being placed in prison before earning his high school diploma or the African American female becoming pregnant before securing hers.

Any attempt to explain the social and cultural fac-tors behind the rise of out-of-wedlock teen pregnan-cies must begin with the fact that most teenage preg-nancies are reportedly unwanted. Eighty-two percent of premarital pregnancies in 15-to-19-year-olds were unwanted.[3] It is mind-boggling how early they become sexually active and how sexually misinformed they are. Many still believe they can't become pregnant during the first six months of sexual activity. Large numbers of teenagers are inconsistent with contraceptives.

I observed one talk show where the mother actually allowed her daughter to have intercourse in her house. Her rationale was she at least knew the child's whereabouts. It's amazing that mothers working away from home are often more effective in monitoring their children's actions and whereabouts from an office telephone than parents who remain at home.

How can a working mother be more effective in monitoring her children's behavior than a welfare mother who is at home all day? How can a working mother achieve more productivity with homework and chores than a mother who is at home?

This epidemic of out-of-wedlock teen pregnancy has created what I call the "chain of pain" that social workers have had difficulty breaking. Listed below are the links in this chain.

Chain of Pain

Low self-esteem
Sexually active adolescents
Lack of prenatal care
Mother consuming drugs while pregnant
Infant mortality
Low birth rate
Out-of-wedlock conception
Adoption
Child neglect
Child abuse
Child abandonment
Welfare
Failing kindergarten
Special education placement

Remedial reading
Suspensions
Poor parental involvement
Lack of neighborhood recreational, educational and
cultural activities
Negative peer pressure
Gangs
Drug-infested neighborhoods
Crime
Homicide
Incarceration
Low life expectancy

The chain of pain is financially and emotionally
costly. Social workers are burning out as they attempt
to break the chain. In my workshops with social workers I remind them that the weakest link of any chain
would be either at the beginning or the end. All other
links are joined together. I have found one of the most
effective strategies to avoid burnout is to practice prevention and intervene before problems begin or at the
earliest stages.

The best way to address teenage pregnancy is to
enhance self-esteem and assess why teens are sexually active. Why does America lead the world in teen
pregnancy? What is it about "First World' America's
values? Why does it lead the world in teen pregnancy,
drug usage, incarceration, handgun possession, homicide, suicide and divorce? Could there be a relationship between America's media that promote sexuality and its high teen pregnancy rate? Conduct your
own survey of weekly TV shows and movies. Count the
number of sexual acts among married people versus

those who are single. Why is single sex glorified over married sex? Why does the advertising industry use sex to sell cars, beer and any other product? Why do most sex education programs exclude abstinence? Many sex education programs have become clinics and condom and Norplant distribution centers.

One of the major reasons why European countries have a lower teen pregnancy rate is because contraceptives historically have been more readily available and their media are less sexually saturated. It does not negate that children and teenagers have a right to know that sex and marriage still go together. We are losing the war on teen pregnancy and drugs because we're not teaching our children values and teaching them that their body is their temple and it belongs to God.

A professional woman's organization that I will leave nameless chose to adopt a group of teenage girls who had given birth out of wedlock. Their objective was to motivate them not to repeat the behavior. They hired a doctor to teach the girls sexuality without abstinence being included. When the girls became pregnant again, the organization grew frustrated and dropped the program. Was the problem solely with the girls? If African American professional women can't save our girls, who can? What will this organization do next?

Magic Johnson had to be reminded, after he had been positively diagnosed as having HIV, to clarify his definition of "safe sex." His original definition, like so many of these programs, was predicated on contraceptives. Later, he rescinded his position and said safe sex is abstinence until marriage.

In my workshops I remind young and older people that because of AIDS and other sexually transmitted diseases, you no longer sleep with a person, you sleep with their history. I inform them that everyone your mate has slept with is also your partner. In mathematical terms, if your mate has been involved with five people over the past two or three years, you are also involved with five persons. If those five were involved with five others, you are now involved with 25 people. If you take that to the next two exponents, you actually are having sex with 625 people! I tease my audience and tell them that before they have sex with anyone they should secure their sexual resume and three references!

Previously I mentioned that 82 percent of all teen pregnancies are unwanted. This statistic is being carefully scrutinized because many young African American mothers indicated they wanted the child and in more extensive interviews felt childbirth was the best they could achieve in life. I tell teenagers you're not at risk because you're low income from a single-parent home. Rather, they are at risk when they don't have goals. When girls are college and career bound, they have less chance of becoming pregnant as a teenager.

The problem teenagers have with goals is that they're based on long-term gratification. The rainbow appears after eight years of elementary school, four years of high school and four years of college. If African American females have not been convinced that a lucrative career awaits them, they may choose to cash in their chips before their 16th birthday and have a child. Two of the most effective strategies to reduce teen pregnancy are teaching abstinence and goal development. In my presentations, I have girls recite: "diploma first, degree second, career third, husband fourth and baby last."

Young girls often say that they decided to have a baby because they wanted someone to love them. They wanted someone to hold and wanted to be needed. Remember many of our girls have never been hugged by a man. Instead, they've been played with by boys. Sixty percent of teen mothers were impregnated by males who were five years older.[4] These boys possess a "weak rap." If they had a stronger rap, they would talk to females their own age. Young naive girls believe that their developing bodies make them women and attractive to men.

Many girls are looking for a man to love them and fill the void of a missing father. They were very much aware before sexual intercourse that these males had no intention of staying. Many girls have decided that since attending college and becoming a professional are unlikely goals, they will instead have a child who needs and loves them.

Many females literally view their babies as dolls. You have to remind these young girls that babies, unlike dolls, cry, their diapers need to be changed, they need to be fed. Unlike dolls that you can place in a corner when you want to go to school or attend a basketball game, or a party, babies are spontaneous, demanding and your permanent responsibility. Many schools use "doll therapy" to help prevent teen pregnancy. They have females care for the doll as if it was a baby for several days.

I look at the women around me, in my family, on my staff and in the larger population. Many of them have expressed a desire to have children but at the appropriate time, when finances, education, career or marital goals are met. It never ceases to amaze me how gainfully employed women feel they cannot afford a child, while others, who are unemployed, and lack a high school diploma, and a husband, do not have any problems having children.

Should we surmise then that the first group understands how to use contraceptives better than the second group? Or that the first group is more sexually responsible than the second? Is there a relationship between sexual responsibility and self-actualization? Could the responsibility that some women show in their sex life spill over into their marriage, education, career and finances? I believe the answer is "yes." I believe the irresponsibility that we see among some men and women in their sexual activities is also evident in their marital, educational, employment and financial pursuits.

Often, irresponsible women and men blame others for their circumstances or say "it just happened." This reminds me of children who when asked where are the cookies that were in the cookie jar, respond with "I don't know." This irresponsibility did not begin at 18 but began very early in the preschool and primary grades.

The psychiatrist and author Frances Welsing suggests that to achieve liberation we should not get married until we first feel good about ourselves, which may take until we're at least 28 years old. We should then allow ourselves two years to get to know one another before having children. Therefore we should wait until 30 to have children. We should only bring into the world that number of children that we can optimally take care of, and Welsing recommends two. Lastly, in order to insure that each child receives enough "lap time," and I would also add that to avoid having two children in college simultaneously, we should spread them four years apart. The key numbers for the maximization of the Black family are 28, 30, 2 and 4.[5] Unfortunately, what is presently going on among many of our families is 0, 13, 5 and 1. We are not marrying, having babies at 13 and having five children one year apart.

We also have the wrong numbers for our grandmothers and great-grandmothers. When I was growing up it was an honor for someone to say that your grandmother really looked nice for her age. Unfortunately, we now live in a culture where it's conceivable to have a 13-year-old mother, a 26-year-old grandmother, a 39-year-old great grandmother and a 52-year-old great, great grandmother. I guess you should look as good as a 26-year-old grandmother and a 39-year-old great grandmother and a 52-year-old great, great grandmother. What used to be an earned honor goes to women through negligence and default.

African American grandmothers play an important role in the day-to-day lives of their children and grandchildren. Grandmothers are more likely to be involved when families are poor and female headed and the grandmother resides with her children and grandchildren. Grandmothers have been found in a variety of parenting roles ranging from the primary parent to the baby-sitter. Almost 44 percent of grandmothers actually had grandchildren residing with them.[6]

Two of the strengths of the African American family have been the extended family component and the multi-generational aspect. In past generations, grandparents were older and more mature. Many of them were retired, and most were grounded in the Lord. In an earlier chapter we cited the percentage decline in church attendance. I believe one contributing factor is the lack of spiritual development among younger and less mature grandmothers.

Many grandmothers are holding their daughters accountable for their sexual activities. They are refusing to be the primary parent and are only providing supplemental assistance. More research is needed in this area, but the assumption seems to be that when grandparents are the primary caretakers, chances are more children are coming soon. This is a very sensitive point. We don't want to deny the mother the opportunity to complete her education and to be gainfully employed. However, mothers must assume the responsibility of rearing their children.

In talking with teen mothers nationwide, I hear more and more of them making a distinction between having a child and having a husband. We've reached an impasse in our culture where some people don't necessarily feel marriage and children go together. Almost 70 percent of our children do not live with both parents. These teenage girls have not eliminated their desire to have children, but they have psychologically eliminated their need for a husband.

On one talk show, a 14-year-old girl had an obsession with wanting to have a baby, but did not have a desire to have a husband nor did she mind going on welfare. I mind that I have to pay taxes for her! Clearly these girls are unaware of the cost of being a parent.

In our rites of passage program for girls we have them review copies of a hospital bill for child delivery. One bill reflects the cost of an average two-day stay in a hospital to give birth to a normal child. This bill averages $3,000. We then show them a hospital bill for a child who had poor prenatal care and was born with a low birth weight. This bill exceeds $30,000. The welfare-dependent mother has no idea or appreciation of this cost, or how it is going to be paid. The bill will be paid by the American taxpayer.

Unlike the Republican Party, I do not want to eliminate welfare, which is only 3 percent of the federal budget, compared to defense and prisons, which exceed 50 percent. My concern is how welfare is being used by some to increase their irresponsibility. What would this girl do before becoming sexually active, if welfare was nonexistent or required learnfare and workfare restrictions?

Welfare provisions have been a major influence in the decline of two-adult households in American cities. Unfortunately, in the African American community, many mothers have decided that a welfare check is actually larger and more stable than the economic resources of an African American man or a minimum wage job. In the last chapter, we talked about the distinction between male income and male image. We live in a materialistic society and many women have chosen income over image and welfare over a man.

Groups like the National Black Social Workers, Children's Defense Fund, and Black Child Development Institute have advocated consistently that the remedy is not welfare but jobs. We need employment that provides wages that exceed the cost of rent, food, childcare, transportation, and medical benefits.

Most mothers prefer employment over welfare, but it is very difficult to expect a person who receives $500 a month in combination of AFDC, food stamps, medical benefits and possibly a housing subsidy to give that up to earn $5 an hour and pay housing, food, childcare, transportation and medical benefits. The issue is not welfare but jobs that pay above the poverty level.

Many mothers, like Aisha in chapter 1, continue to chose below-poverty wages over welfare because of their extreme desire to become self-sufficient. Other mothers have attempted to merge the two together and supplement their meager welfare benefits with outside entrepreneurial activities. The government says they want initiative, but penalizes anyone who earns extra income.

We must provide research that empowers low income single mothers. Reginald Clark, in the significant book *Family Life in School Achievement,* provides helpful information. His research included both single and two parent homes from both low-income and middle-class backgrounds. He concludes the most important variables were not the *number* of parents or the *income,* but the *quality* of the interaction. Parents who transmit hope, are consistent, are complimentary, give high expectations and believe they are the primary educator were more successful regardless of marital status and income.[7]

My desire is not to promote single parenting, but I do believe you have to play the hand you're dealt to the best of your ability. There are some advantages to being a single parent. They include:

- one decision maker
- less inconsistency
- greater bonding
- greater quality time
- greater self-development

In many two-parent families, the father has one rule and the mother has another. Consequently, children take advantage of this inconsistency. In single-parent homes there's only one parent to make the decision. Therefore the only inconsistency would be when the parent has one rule on Monday and another on Wednesday which is also applicable in two-parent homes. I have observed that the bond between a single mother and a child, especially a male child, is often greater than the bond that exists between the mother and a new spouse. Children see spouses come and go, but the relationship between parent and child is forever.

When both spouses are present, they often spend more time with one another thereby reducing the amount of time that either parent can spend with a child. In a single-parent home, parents can allocate all of their time to their children excluding time for themselves. If two parents give two hours each, it's equivalent to one parent who gives four, but the bond between the parent that gave four hours to their child will probably be greater. Single parents not only have the opportunity to allocate more time to their children, but also more time to their own growth and development. Many single mothers expressed that when they were married, their husbands did not encourage them to pursue education, entrepreneurship, and/or hobbies. I chose to write about the advantages of single parenting first because the media do an excellent job of delineating the disadvantages. Listed below are some of them:

> Less income available
> 50% greater chance that an adult will not be on the premises
> Less energy to discipline, tutor and nurture
> The missing gender role model and perspective
> Loneliness

Due to sexism, a single female parent will earn one third as much as a two-parent family. A married couple has a 100 percent greater chance of having one adult at home, thus reducing the possibility of teen pregnancy. A single parent who has worked an eight-hour day plus commuting, cooking, washing dishes and cleaning the house will have less energy available to discipline, tutor and nurture. Children can help and learn responsibility simultaneously. When children do not have both parents present, they miss the perspective of the absent parent and also miss the role model image that they're either going to grow up to be like or a criterion for choosing a mate.

Lastly, being a single parent is often lonely, when you're watching your child walk, ride their bicycle, or read for the first time and there is no one to share the experience. There is a distinction between single *parenting* and being a single *parent*. The former is a process and the latter is a position. A mother can be a single parent, but she does not have to rear her children by herself. She can draw upon the rich reservoir of the extended family. We cited earlier the tremendous contributions that grandmothers make to the development of their children. In addition, mothers can draw upon their father, brothers, uncles, cousins, nephews, pastor, coworkers, neighbors and friends. Because single parenting is on the increase, more and more single parents are networking to assist and empower each other.

Initially, when I was doing the outline for this book, this particular chapter was called "teen pregnancy." Later it was changed to "single parenting" and ultimately to balance "fatherhood," it was titled "Motherhood." Therefore, I would be remiss if I didn't discuss motherhood within the context of a father being present. While it only happens 34 percent of the time in African American families, this is God's design to raise children. We need to advocate for the rich experience of motherhood with a supportive husband.

Motherhood, when it's done right, is supported by a loving husband who is attentive to her needs throughout the nine months of pregnancy. They attend classes together. He nurtures her and makes her feel beautiful and special while her body is ever changing. He treats her like a queen. He believes she is a "Proverbs 31 woman." He's by her side in the delivery room, ready to hold her hand, and provide reassurance. He drives her home from the hospital and makes sure she and the baby are comfortable. Ideal motherhood allows her to stay home indefinitely to nurture, breastfeed and read to her child. He is able to provide a comfortable standard of living that does not require her to work up to the day of delivery and return to the office in six weeks. Optimally, the mother can choose to stay home six weeks, six months or six years with full support of her husband. He has given her a seed and she has given him a child.

We have explored marriage, fatherhood, and motherhood. The following chapter will describe the development of our children.

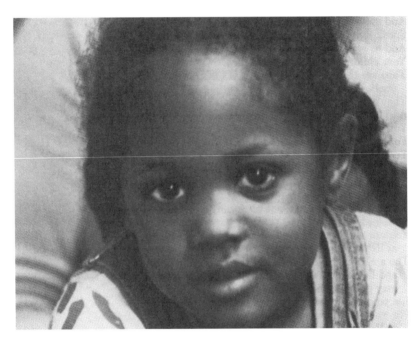

Children are the Reward of Life.

CHAPTER SIX

CHILDHOOD

roverbs 22: 6. *Train up a child in the way he should go and when he is old he will not depart from it.*

Deuteronomy 6: 7. *You shall teach them diligently to your children and shall talk of them when you sit in your house. When you walk by the way, when you lie down and when you rise up.*

Ephesians 6:1. *Children obey your parents and the Lord for this is right. Honor your father and your mother which is the first commandment with promise.*

Proverbs 13: 24. *He who spares his rod hates his son, but he who loves him, disciplines him promptly.*

New King James Translation

Former Surgeon General Jocelyn Elders says that too many of our children suffer from the five H's: hugless, helpless, homeless, hopeless and hunger. Abraham Maslow wrote that it's very difficult to transcend higher levels of human growth when basic needs such as clean water, food, clothing, shelter, health and safety have not been provided. Presently, one third of African American families and 50 percent of our children live below the poverty line.[1] These children are at great risk of suffering from one or more of these five H factors.

It becomes difficult, if not impossible, for a class-room teacher to move a child to a higher level of growth and development if the child is hungry. Many of our children consume not their best meals, but their *only* two meals during the school breakfast and lunch pro-gram. Many schools and agencies have had to con-tinue the food program beyond the school year and into the summer. Our crime watch group provides dinner for wayward boys. The ultimate desire is to move our children to a higher level of growth and development.

Many of our children are without a permanent resi-dence. They live with their parents in boarding houses, transient hotels and on the streets. There are 50,000 African American children who need to be adopted.[2] A disproportionate number of these children are adoles-cent males. What are teachers to do when children are hungry and homeless?

While some of our children suffer from too little, others suffer from materialism. These children own everything from telephones, televisions, VCRs, stereo systems, and video game systems to miniature refrig-erators and microwave ovens. This generation might be the first to never leave home. After all, it makes more sense to stay in their private penthouse apart-ment, without any financial responsibility, than to go out into the world and make it on their own.

This dichotomy in our community reminds me of when I went to Ghana several years ago. I was struck by the similarity of living conditions suffered by chil-dren living in the "third world" and "first world." The myth is that it's better to live in America than Africa, but I didn't see much difference.

Electricity and indoor plumbing are provided in the urban areas of Ghana, but in the rural areas poverty is extreme and electricity and plumbing are nonexistant. While I saw more poverty in rural Ghana, I observed tightly knit families who loved each other. I wondered what did they do in the evening without electricity. They told me they shared stories, sang songs, danced and played the drum around the fire. Many of us would think that would be primitive, but when you look at "first world" America, many parents are afraid to let their children play outside, sit on the porch, or near a window inside their house. Is this not primitive and backward? Our children are safer in Ghana than America.

In "third world" Africa, an ancient rites of passage program is still in place, teaching boys and girls how to become men and women. In "first world" Ame rica it is not clear when boys and girls become men and women. African American children have developed their own criteria for manhood and womanhood, which may include materialism, drug consumption, sexual promiscuity, pregnancy, gang involvement, and becoming incarcerated.

Another tremendous challenge in childhood is securing a sound academic background. Many parents are forced to choose between safety and academics. Many of them choose safety. Unfortunately, many African American parents have to choose between sending their child to a neighborhood public school that is gang and drug infested, but has a larger number of African American teachers who hopefully will provide more nurturance, higher expectations, and Africentricity, or a private suburban school that might be safer, but lacks African American teachers, students, and a Africentric curriculum.

The million-dollar questions that so many parents ask me are, Where should they send their children to school - inner city, suburbs, neighborhood, boarding, or home school? What type of school is best - public, private, Catholic, Africentric, or magnet? While parents have to make their own decision in the child's best interest, I do think it's hypocritical for public school teachers to send their children to private schools and be against low-income parents having access for their children through vouchers.

I once counseled a suburban parent who told me her options were to send her child to the neighborhood school, which only had one African American teacher, who told her the school would break her son's spirit, or send him across the same tracks that they had just left to the inner city school infested by gangs, drugs and violence, but had a 70 percent African American teaching staff and an Africentric curriculum. An African American superintendent told me there were 400 African American children who had graduated from the junior high schools, but only 21 of them graduated from the high school. Not even mobility can explain losing 379 students.

Some parents have chosen to send their children to private school, even with the tremendous financial strain. Some send their children to boarding schools which are more expensive and can also be emotionally damaging to children. Some parents send their children to neighborhood schools and supplement themselves or send them to evening and Saturday cultural and academic programs. My company has operated one for over a decade. Other parents have decided they will homeschool their children.

Some parents think they have a formula on how to matriculate their children through the malaise of White supremacy. Their plan is to send their child to a White elementary school, a Black high school and a White college. They believe in the theory of alternation. Other parents will send their children to all-White schools throughout. They believe in the theory of White supremacy and acculturation. Others enroll their children in all-White elementary and high schools for a strong academic foundation, but send them to a Black college for their history and culture. They believe in the theory of multiculturalism. Other parents send their children to all-Black elementary and high schools to ground them in their history and culture and then to an all-White college so they can compete in White corporate America. They believe in the theory of integration.

I'm amazed at these formulas, and they are based on some even more amazing premises: the erroneous assumption that Black schools are only good for culture, but not for academics, and White schools are academically sound, but lacking in infusing Africentricity into the curriculum.

Segregated Black schools in 1930 had a illiteracy rate of 20 percent while in 2000 after integration it was 44 percent. Children are passed from one grade to another without acquiring the grade-appropriate skills due to social promotion. Ironically, the quality African American studies programs are at White universities. Some Black colleges don't feel Africentricity should be part of their curriculum.

All parents want their children in a safe, academically, and culturally stimulating school environment as close to their home as possible. Unfortunately if our generation does not provide those institutions, then our children will be wrestling with the same issues for their children.

I mentioned in an earlier chapter that increasing literacy rates may be the best strategy to prevent other social ills that are manifesting in the African American community. I believe one of the best ways to reduce the number of African American males in the penal system is to teach them how to read. Another prevention approach is for parents to spend more time with their children. In agrarian societies, parents spent literally the entire day with their children. Today, the average father spends seven minutes and the average mother only 34 minutes per day talking to their children.[3] Every effort should be made to increase the amount of time we are spending with our children.

In my earlier book, *To Be Popular or Smart: The Black Peer Group*, I indicated that in 1950 the greatest influence on children was the home, followed by school and church. In 2000, the greatest influences are the peer group, rappers, and television respectively.[4] I believe whoever spends the most time with our children will have the greatest influence.

I propose that there is a science to being a parent. Following, is a parental checklist. Try the following exercise: take the test, grading yourself from A to F, then have your children take the test. Compare answers.

Grades

_____ Have you taught your children about God, His word and the power of prayer?

_____ Do your children have goals?

_____ Do you provide quality time?

_____ Do you praise more than you criticize?

_____ How well do you listen to your children?

_____ Are you consistent?

_____ Do you give them high expectations?

_____ Do you teach your children African history?

_____ Have you provided your children with a nutritious diet?

_____ Do you monitor homework?

_____ Do you select, discuss and monitor television shows?

_____ Do you know your children's friends and their values?

_____ Could your children develop a family tree?

_____ Do your children receive adequate sleep?

_____ Do you take your children on field trips?

_____ How frequently do you visit your child's school?

_____ Do you listen and discuss your children's music selections?

_____ How disciplined are your children?

_____ How well do your children complete chores?

_____ How frequently do you touch your children?

_____ Have you provided a safe environment for your children?

Please honestly grade yourself in the above areas. What can you do to improve? Where are the schools that teach us how to parent? How will we learn? For many of us it is from trial and error, repeating what we learned from our parents.

Do you take your children on field trips to museums and other educational institutions? Some White parents who live hundreds of miles away visit museums in the Black community. We often claim financial hardship, but many of these institutions are free. We need to evaluate our priorities and values. Principals and teachers often tell me African American parents claim to be broke and can't contribute to the field trip, while puffing on a cigarette! As a race, we're guilty of buying what we want and begging for what we need.

What are the contents of your house? More than anything else, your furnishings tell much about your values, and ultimately tell what type of child you are raising. I believe there are homes designed to produce dropouts, drug dealers, rappers, athletes, ministers, doctors, engineers, and teachers. What type of person is your home designed to produce? Is your home designed to produce children with an Africentric or Eurocentric consciousness?

The typical American home has three televisions, two CD players, 200 cassettes, four stereo systems, two VCR's, and plenty of liquor bottles and cigarettes. The one book in the house - the Bible—stays open, but is not read. A more academically and culturally stimulating home will have a Bible or Qu'ran, pictures of Black people on the walls, and Africentric books for children and adults. They have library cards, paper, pencils, pens, calculator, scrabble, chess, checkers, a globe, an atlas, a computer, a musical instrument, a microscope and a chemistry set. Does your house reflect the first or second scenario?

For the past decade, Jesse Jackson has been imploring African American parents to do five things:

1) Walk your child to school and on the first day meet your child's teacher.

2) Exchange telephone numbers with the teacher.

3) Monitor children's homework.

4) Pick up your child's report card.

5) Turn off the television two hours in the evening and study.

Parents should watch television together with their children or at least determine what they should watch. Identify shows that teach morals and character development such as *Cosby, Little House on the Prairie, Highway to Heaven* and *Touched by an Angel.*

Parents only have 18 years to develop children. My two sons are now adults and I am a living witness, time passes very quickly. Today, our children are growing faster than ever before. As discussed in my book, *Developing Positive Self Images and Discipline in Black Children,* and by Neil Postman in *The Disappearance of Childhood,* our children are being robbed of their innocence. The leading culprits are children's overexposure to television, a protein-concentrated diet and a high-tech economy.

Not such a long time ago, information was mostly acquired through the written word. Today, our children learn mostly from television. They assume that since they watch what we watch, they know what we know. I cringe when I see parents allowing their children to watch "R" rated movies filled with violence, sex, and profanity.

One distinction between adulthood and childhood is shame. Children who are innocent possess shame. As children increasingly watch more violent and sexual acts from birth until 18 years old they begin to lose their innocence, shame, and childhood. There can be no childhood when there is no shame.

Our children are growing too fast - literally. This is the first generation of children almost completely raised on cow's milk rather than being breastfed. All animals are equipped to feed their young, but only human mothers use bottles. Cow's milk is designed for calves and develops the body. Human's milk develops the brain. Children are starting their menstrual cycle six months earlier, little girls as young as eight are beginning their menstrual periods because of cow's milk and excessive red meat in their diets.[5] You can't distinguish high-school girls from their teachers.

The last culprit is a high-tech service-oriented economy that delays young adults from being financially self-sufficient. In earlier generations, a man could economically provide for his family by working on a farm at age 14 or in a factory at age 16. In this current economy it may take until you're 28 years of age to be economically self-sufficient. What is a youth to do with a mind overexposed to television, an overdeveloped body from protein and the economy that says wait ten years?

Our children are like clay, and we are the potters. Parents have a tremendous responsibility to develop their children's talents. There is a direct relationship between parental involvement and children's development. Thus teachers must assist schools in maximizing parental involvement.

Young immature parents will require workshops for their self-esteem, male-female relationships and job training. We must encourage involvement by providing incentives such as transportation, child care, a door prize, food, and their children performing.

The following chapter will discuss raising our children under value systems other than Eurocentrism, materialism, and individualism. Clearly, they are not working. It used to be that the Ku Klux Klan was our greatest threat, but today we're challenged by another KKK: Kids Killing Kids. We must change our children's values.

Our children's values are being shaped by advertising.

CHAPTER SEVEN

VALUES: THE KEYS TO THE FAMILY

*No servant can be the slave of two masters;
he will hate one and love the other;
he will be loyal to one and despise
the other. You cannot serve
both God and money.*
Luke 16:13. *Good News Translation.*

Can you imagine traveling cross country without a map? Can you fathom being an inexperienced cook attempting to prepare a complex dish without a recipe? Would you try to assemble a piece of equipment with over 100 parts without referring to the instructions? Can you imagine trying to stay married and raise children without values and morals? Many Americans and specifically African Americans are trying to do just that. We are trying to develop and build families without a map, recipe, directions and values.

In Chapter Two I introduced the terms "third world" and "first world." What makes America first? The fact that it leads the world in homicide, divorce, incarceration, hand gun possession and drug usage? America is considered first because of its gross national product. What cannot be explained mathematically is how the United States with 4 percent of the world's population consumes 60 percent of all the drugs.[1] Or consider the following:

---

Deaths by handguns

10 Australia
13 Sweden
22 Britain
68 Canada
87 Japan
19,000 United States[2]

Scripture reminds us that you can't serve two masters. Does America value God or money? I believe the best way to measure a culture is to observe how well it respects its elders, women, children, and teachers. America fails in all four areas. On the other hand, in so-called primitive Africa, elders are highly respected, children are the reward of life, women are viewed as the creators of life, and teachers are revered because no career can be learned without one.

Listed below are some of the dichotomies between African and American values.

African	American
We	I
Cooperation	Competition
Internal	External
Extended Family	Nuclear family
Village	Solo parenting
Spiritualism	Materialism

After 1954 and integration we were finally able to attend White schools, buy from White and live in White neighborhoods. Gradually, we immersed ourselves and became inculcated with a Eurocentric value system.

Earlier in the book I mentioned that the two greatest problems facing the African American family are separation from God and unemployment. I believe an Africentric value system can return us to God and make our people more economically productive.

We will explore three value systems in this chapter: Maat, sometimes called the Declarations of Innocence or the Negative Confessions that were developed approximately 2527 BC; The Ten Commandments that were developed approximately 1300 BC;[3] and the Nguzo Saba developed in 1966. These value systems have African origins and are interrelated. Africa's gross national product does not exceed America's, but when it comes to contributions in the realm of moral and spiritual development, Africa is far more advanced than America. Listed below are the cardinal virtues of Maat, the Ten Commandments and the Nguzo Saba.

Maat

Truth
Justice
Order
Harmony
Balance
Righteousness/Propriety
Reciprocity

The Ten Commandments

Thou shalt have no other God before Me.
Thou shalt not bow down to any idol of worship.
Do not make for yourself images of anything in heaven or on earth.
Observe the Sabbath and keep it holy.

Respect your father and your mother.
Do not commit murder .
Do not commit adultery.
Do not steal.
Do not accuse anyone falsely.
Do not desire another man's wife.

Nguzo Saba

Umoja - unity
Kujichagulia - self-determination
Ujima - collective work and responsibility
Ujamaa - cooperative economics
Nia - purpose
Kuumba - creativity
Imani - faith

There is a direct relationship between Maat and the Ten Commandments. The latter are drawn from the former. They both originated in Egypt. During Moses's stay in Egypt he was exposed to the principles of Maat. The Ten Commandments are simply a continuation of its legacy. Maulana Karenga in 1966 drew upon the African tradition in developing the Nguzo Saba.

African value systems are to be lived everyday, not just celebrated for seven days, then shelved the rest of the year. We must begin to eat, sleep, and drink the principles of Maat, the Nguzo Saba, and the Ten Commandments. We must become comfortable in pronouncing Kiswahili words, and we must go beyond rote memorization of a few key phrases. Most African Americans know the Ten Commandments by heart. And since Maat is still new to many of us, we should begin to study, memorize, and apply.

I am imploring African American people to raise their families with these values. It is also my desire to make these values as concrete and visible as possible. Since the Nguzo Saba and Maat are relatively new to African Americans, the following discussion is designed to help you understand how they can be applied to everyday life.

Maat

Truth. There was once a family having two brothers, ages eight and ten. They had been playing in the garage while their parents were upstairs in the house. There were many items in the garage including toys and their father's tools and equipment. After the boys had played for an hour with their toys, they began to play with some of their father's tools and equipment. Accidentally, they poured gasoline that ordinarily went into the snowblower into the lawnmower, which contained a combination of gas and oil. Later that day, when their father needed to use the lawnmower he was unable to start it. He asked his sons if they knew anything about it. The two boys looked guilty at each other and the father knew they'd done something wrong. He reminded them that it is one thing to do something wrong, but it is far greater to lie about it. He reminded his sons there was a lesser punishment for breaking the lawnmower than lying. He told them that there's nothing he valued more than the truth. The boys looked at each other again and decided it was time to tell the truth.

Justice. The questions that African people have been asking God for a long time are, why is it that wherever Europeans are in the world, they are in control?

How can less than 15 percent of the world's population control most of the world's resources? How could a minority population invade Africa and control the population and the land? Why were African people forced to leave their homeland? Why were family members separated from one another during slavery? Why were African people forced to work for free from 1619 to 1865? Why were so many White Americans given cheap and free land while African people were never given their 40 acres, mule and $50.00. Why were so many Africans lynched? Why would God allow so many African women to be raped by White men? How can 1 percent of the American population own 48 percent of the wealth and 10 percent own 86 percent?[4] Scripture says, God will not be mocked. He is always on the side of the oppressed. It has been said that oppression and challenges make you strong. God is on the side of the oppressed. That may explain why God placed the chosen people on Earth first. God wants justice, fairness, peace, and equitable distribution of resources.

Order. One of the major problems for American families and particularly African American families is that there is no order in the home. Even in nuclear families there seems to be a lack of order in the decision making process. The American family became more liberal as they began to watch shows like *Different Strokes* that had children talking back to their parents and parents wearing their children's clothes and attending the same events. Children now tell parents when they will return. Parents now ask children for money. Spouses disrespect each other and speak in hostile tones. The natural order of the family is described in Ephesians 5:21-28.

God   Father   Mother   Children

The proper family order noted above was not listed in a hierarchical or vertical manner intentionally. The horizontal layout shows the complementary relationship between family members. In an earlier chapter on marriage, I mentioned that the father is the head of the house, but God is the head of his life. The father has the ultimate decision making authority, but he will consult with his wife and both will respect their children. This is God's order.

Harmony. There had been a lot of shouting in the household this morning. Everyone seemed to be angry and hostile with one another. A smile had not been seen in this house for the past week. The words "thank you" and "I'm sorry" had gone on vacation. Praise and compliments were on sabbatical. The mother had grown tired of hollering. She remembered one of the cardinal virtues of Maat was harmony. She reminded her family that from this day on, no one would allowed to raise their voice or holler at anyone else again. She also decreed that criticism of the person would no longer be tolerated - only criticism of the behavior. She said in the spirit of harmony we will praise each other more. Harmony is peaceful.

Balance. It had been a long day for Joanne. She had risen at 5:00 a.m., made breakfast and lunch for the family and was out of the house by 7:00 a.m. in order to be at work at 8:00 a.m. Later that evening, after a long grueling day at work, Joanne came home to be greeted by a heavy level of gloom. Her three boys were sitting on one sofa, eating popcorn with their feet on the table. Half the popcorn was on the carpet. Her husband was in his favorite rocking chair drinking a beer. "Hi, baby." "Hi, mom," then "what's for dinner?" they asked. She decided instantly to-night she would teach them about balance. Women are not placed on earth to be man's servant. She reminded them that they all lived in the house, and they all needed to keep it clean. Balance means sharing the chores. Balance means that women's work is not al-ways on the inside and man's work always on the out-side. She listed all the chores that are required to main-tain a household and then divided those chores by five.

Reciprocity. Raynard and Renee had been seeing each other for the past two months. After several dates they had grown fond of each other. Soon they'd have to make a critical decision on the future of their rela-tionship and their level of commitment. During dinner, Raynard told Renee that he wanted her to be his lady. Renee had decided not to pressure Raynard and she wanted him to make the decision. This was her desire after the third date, but she knew from previous expe-rience if you force a partner to make a commitment before he's ready, he may run away. She asked Raynard what did it mean to be his lady. He said, she didn't need to date anyone else. Renee then asked Raynard in the spirit of reciprocity, if the same rule applied for him? Raynard became quiet and began to fidget in the chair. He said, "I want you to be my lady, but a man has to be a man. You're my number one lady, but from time to time I'll need space to see somebody else." Renee then calmly responded, in the spirit of reciprocity, that what is good for the goose is good for the gander.

Righteousness/Propriety. William and Sharon had been seeing each other for six months. They enjoyed talking to each other and had similar interests. They attended book parties, plays and concerts together. They loved going out to dinner and listening to jazz. Sharon noticed that William wanted to spend the night more and more. The first time it happened she agreed because it was 3:00 a.m. Sunday morning, and she thought it was too late for William to drive home. Soon William would negotiate staying over as early as 7:00 p.m. in the evening. She also noticed that William was leaving more and more of his clothes and personal items at her apartment.

She had talked to her girlfriends, many of whom were already shacking with their boyfriends. Sharon had mixed feelings about this arrangement. She had been raised in a strong Christian home where that behavior was unacceptable. She felt violated because it was her apartment and William should have asked before he left his things. She decided she would have a long conversation tonight with William about righteousness and how the Lord feels about this lifestyle.

Nguzo Saba

Unity. The big day had finally arrived. The media had used every trick they had in their arsenal to divide and conquer, but on October 16, 1995, a million African American men with different religions, ideologies, economic backgrounds, and educational levels managed to put aside their differences. They had come from Japan, London, the Caribbean, and America. They left the violence behind to stand for

123

peace. Over one million brothers stood next to each other, brushed up against each other, stepped on each other's shoes, hugged each other, communicated with each other, and unity was the motivating force. They put aside their differences and accentuated their commonalities.

Self-determination. I have enjoyed watching my sons grow into manhood. I remember when the youngest son first learned how to ride a two-wheel bicycle. He tried to convince me that he could only ride a bicycle with training wheels. He told me he could never ride a two-wheel bicycle. Later, he would have difficulties with his math homework and he'd try to convince me that he could never solve the problems. I remember when he first got into a swimming pool and told me how afraid he was of the water. I taught him the principle of self-determination and shortly afterwards in each of those occasions, he learned how to ride a two-wheel bicycle, mastered his math problems, and he became a fish in the water. We must remove the word "can't" from our vocabulary and replace it with self-determination.

Collective work and responsibility. It was Saturday morning and everybody in the Davis house knew their chores. As they anxiously prepared themselves for the big party later that afternoon, each person was assigned a task such as mopping, vacuuming, dusting, washing windows, decorating, and cooking. What should happen if one person finishes before another? Have you ever finished your chores before someone in your household? Have you ever volunteered to help someone in the house who hadn't finished their work?

Have you ever volunteered to help someone hoping that they would not accept your offer? Always remember in the spirit of Ujima none of us are finished doing our work until all of us are finished doing our work.

Cooperative economics. I read about the Evans family in New Jersey almost a decade ago. Some families only get together at funerals. They say they want to get together more frequently for family reunions, scholarships, and other worthwhile family projects. Most of it's just talk. The Evans family is different. More than a decade ago, ten of them decided they were going to open a mutual fund. They all agreed they would contribute $100 a month to the fund for a grand total of $1,000. There were some months when it was very difficult for some of the members to raise their $100 but they scuffled and were able to achieve their goals. Had they not believed in cooperative economics, seeds of distrust would have been planted. They now in the spirit of cooperative economics have assets that exceed 2.3 million dollars. Singularly, they would not have amassed this wealth. It took cooperative economics.

Purpose. Daniel was happy. Today was his 12th birthday. His family had sung happy birthday to him, and the cake and ice cream were all ready to be eaten. The most important part of the day was yet to come. The family tradition required that on your birthday you had to set goals for the year. One year, Daniel was not prepared to answer that question and the cake and ice cream were not eaten until the following day when Daniel had finally decided his purpose. Like his mother always said, "You're not at risk because you're

Black, low income, and from a single-parent home. You're at risk when you don't have any goals. His mother reminded him that if he didn't know where he was going, any road would take him there. If you don't know where you're going, the gang members and drug dealers will tell you. In the spirit of Nia what is your purpose?

Creativity. The mission statement and goals for a Chicago theater company states that every African American household should have something African in their homes. This could include an African artifact, clothing, portrait, or a strip of kente cloth. Periodically, family members should also wear African dress. In the childhood chapter I mentioned that the contents of your home reflect your values. Wouldn't it be nice if you could go into every African American home and see a piece of your culture? In the spirit of creativity we must never litter and do always as much as we can in the way we can in order to leave our community more beautiful and beneficial than when we inherited it.

Faith. It's often said that a family that prays together will stay together. This becomes very difficult in a household that reminds you more of an airport or a train station than a home. It becomes even more challenging when fathers only allocate seven minutes, mothers 34 minutes, to spend with their children. When was the last time your family prayed together outside of meal time? When was the last time your family had Bible study? In the spirit of Imani, we must find time for God as a family. We must listen and talk to God through prayer and Scripture.

126

It is my prayer that these three value systems become your guiding light. In Luke 6:46 the Scripture reminds us that we must dig deep and put the foundation on the rock. I pray that all of us, including my own family, dig deep through prayer and Scripture and place our house on Jesus. Unfortunately the Scripture reminds us that even if we do this, the floods will come, but if the house is dug deeply and is on the rock, the house will stand. Any house grounded in Maat, the Ten Commandments and the Nguzo Saba will be able to weather the storm. Unfortunately, many of us have never relied on these principles and our houses are being washed away by the floods. When that happens, the nigger spirit can take over.

Niggers are violent.

CHAPTER EIGHT

THE NIGGER SPIRIT

The Son of Man will die as the Scripture says he will,
but how terrible for that man (Judas) who will
betray the Son of Man! It would have
been better for that man if he
had never been born.
Mark 14:21. *Good News Translation*

Reverend Frank Reid preached a sermon at my church during Men's Week titled The Nigger Spirit.[1] It inspired me so much I wanted to write about how that spirit was created and why it must die. I know nigger is a very inflammatory word, and many conscious African Americans and others who are puritanical about the language have a problem with the use of the word. Let me first define the word from my perspective.

Nigger: someone who is ignorant and who hates himself or herself. The person can be of any race.

Historically only African people have been called nigger, but as you can see my definition encompasses anyone of any race who is ignorant and hates himself. The meaning of the word becomes even more confusing when we call each other by the name, saying "that's my nigger," and yet many become offended, hostile, or want to fight when people outside our race call us by that name.

Frank preached that God made us male and female. God did not make niggers. Two of the major manufacturers of niggers are White supremacy and classism.

White supremacists are niggers because they are ignorant. They believe that their lack of color makes them superior to people who have color.

Unfortunately, oppression also affects the victims of White supremacy, classism, and monopoly capitalism. They begin to internalize self-hatred. The nigger spirit was finetuned when slave owners realized it was more effective to place the chains around the mind rather than the body. The infamous Willie Lynch letter of 1712 on how to make a slave reads as follows:

> Gentlemen: I greet you here on the bank of the James River in the year of our Lord, 1712. First, I shall thank you the gentlemen of the colony of Virginia for bringing me here. I am here to help you solve some of your problems with slaves. You invitation reached me on my modest plantation in the West Indies while experimenting with some of the newest and still oldest methods for control of slaves. Ancient Rome would envy us if my program is implemented. As our boat sails south on the James River, named for illustrious King James, whose Bible we cherish, I find enough to know that your problem is not unique. While Rome used cords of wood as crosses for standing human bodies along the old highways in great numbers, you are here using the tree and rope on occasion. I caught the whiff of a dead slave hanging from a tree a couple of miles back. You're not only losing valuable stock by hangings, you are having uprisings, slaves are running away, your crops are sometimes left in the fields too long for maximum profit, you suffer occasional fires, you're animals are killed, gentlemen, . . . you know what your problems are; I do not need to elaborate. I am not here to method for controlling your black slaves. I guarantee everyone of you that if installed correctly it will control the slave for at

least 300 years. My method is simple, any member of your family or any overseer can use it. I have outlined a number of differences among the slaves and I take these differences and make them bigger. I use fear, mistrust and envy for control purposes. These methods have worked on my modest plantation in the West Indies, and they will work throughout the south. Take this simple little list of differences and think about them. On the top of my list is age, but it is there only because it only starts with A, the second is color or shade, there is intelligence, size, sex, size of plantation, attitude of owners, whether the slaves lived in the valley, on the hill east, west, north, south, have fine or coarse hair, or is tall or short. Now that you have a list of differences, I shall give you an outline of action - but before that, I shall assure you that distrust is stronger than trust, and envy is stronger than adulation, respect or admiration. The black slave, after receiving this indoctrination, shall carry on and become self refueling and self generating for hundreds of years, maybe thousands. Don't forget you must pitch the old black versus the young black male and the young black male against the old black male. You must use the dark skinned slaves versus the light skinned slaves, and the light skinned slaves versus the dark skinned slaves. You must use the female versus the male, and the male versus the female. You must also have your servants and over-seers distrust all blacks, but it is necessary that your slaves trust and depend on us. They must love, respect and trust only us. Gentlemen, these kits are your keys to control, use them, have your wives and children use them. Never miss an opportunity. My plan is guaranteed and the good thing about this plan is that if used intensely for one year, the slaves themselves will remain perpetually distrustful.[2]

Naive Whites refuse to believe the viciousness of the proponents of White supremacy. They are in a state of denial until they read the Willie Lynch letter or watch the Rodney King tape. I was not surprised when Willie Lynch's tricks were used to divide us on the Million Man March. While it did confuse many, hopefully, the tremendous response of a million African men on October 16, 1995, will help us break the nigger mold.

If we are to develop strong African American families and communities we must break the nigger spirit. The following is a list of some nigger traits I have observed:

- Wakes up late.
- Ask, "what's happening" because they don't know.
- Doesn't work.
- Doesn't like to work.
- Arrives late for work.
- Doesn't like working for Black people.
- Doesn't save money.
- Doesn't support Black businesses.
- More concerned about their hairstyle than their brains.
- Spends more money for clothes and cars than the apartment or house.
- Buys more lottery tickets than mutual funds.
- Makes babies, but does not take care of them.
- Calls women "B's."
- Lives in a dirty house.
- Writes on public walls.
- Litters in the neighborhood.
- Urinates in the alley.
- Throws bottles out of cars.
- Engages in destructive behavior.

- Loves watching television.
- Hates reading, especially about African history or big books, prefers picture books.
- Loves to get high.
- Can't party without being high.
- Arrives at programs late.
- Doesn't ask for directions when lost.
- Volunteers to take you somewhere, then runs out of gas.
- Use the term "you know" throughout the sentence because they don't.
- Gossips.
- Exaggerates.
- Can't complete a sentence without cursing, especially the "MF" word.
- Looks for differences.
- Looks for the negative versus the positive.
- Acts like crabs in a barrel.
- Jealous.
- Kill people who look like them.
- Grab their crouch looking for power.

It is going to be very difficult building a strong African family with niggers. It will be challenging employing niggers if they don't want to work, don't like to work, come to work late, and are not willing to work for African Americans. It will be problematic raising capital to build African American businesses if niggers don't save and don't trust each other financially. Its virtually impossible if people spend 97 percent of their money with White businesses.[3] Niggers still believe the White man's water is colder, lemonade sweeter, and their doctors and lawyers are smarter.

Have you ever been to a nigger's house? School restroom? Have you ever driven down niggers' streets where you must dodge broken bottles? Who's responsible for this mess? White people? Do White people live in our homes, write on our school walls, destroy our restrooms, litter, or throw bottles in our neighborhoods? Or was that done by the niggers of our own race? I probably need to be more careful, but there have been numerous times when I've been driving down the street and some nigger in front of me is throwing litter or bottles out of his car. I pull beside him and remind him that is our neighborhood and it is our responsibility to keep it clean. I ask him, Can you blame what you just did on the White man? Niggers look at me like I'm crazy, and my wife is concerned about my safety, but it's the only way I know to kill the nigger spirit.

I love to dance, but I often wonder why niggers who say they love to party have to be high before they dance. If they love to party and the party started at 10:00 p.m. why do they arrive at midnight and then become indignant when the party concludes at 2:00 a.m.?

When I'm scheduled to speak at a certain time it frustrates me to have to wait 30 and 45 minutes for niggers to arrive. I respect the late Elijah Muhammed who said the program will start at 2:00 p.m. regardless of the attendance. I honestly believe one of the reasons why our people are late is because they know the program is not going to start. We penalize those who are prompt and reward latecomers. I believe we could change niggers' behavior if we started on time.

My speaking contract has a clause which states that I'm to be driven by a professional driver. I had to learn the hard way. On one trip a brother volunteered to take me to the airport. Rather than concentrating on the road, he wanted to convert the trip into a mini workshop and engage me in dialogue. The result was a major collision - the car was totaled and his three daughters and the two of us were injured. I have been driven by people who did not have directions and were too egotistical to ask. Others have volunteered to drive me to the airport without gas!

The most glaring problems of niggers are they're jealous, backstab, look for differences, gossip, and cannot be insulted. You can talk about them and they respond. You can take advantage of them and they don't respond. People who are self-actualized can be insulted. In the following chapter, we discuss the need for us to raise our insult level and our expectations of ourselves and our people.

Why are there so many foreign businesses in the Black community?

CHAPTER NINE

INSULT LEVEL

 was inspired to write this chapter after listening to Jesse Jackson challenge his listeners by asking, "what is it that insults you and moves you to action?"

An insult is an indignity, an affront to someone's self-respect. The problem with niggers is that they seldom if ever get insulted. They allow anything to be said and done to them. It has been said that African American people have a high insult level. We accept injustices and seldom call, write, research, protest, demonstrate, organize, boycott, or build institutions.

What injustices have forced you to take a stand? Fannie Lou Hamer said, "I'm sick and tired of being sick and tired." Frederick Douglass said, "Find out just what any people will quietly submit to and you have found out the exact measure of injustice and wrong that will be imposed upon them, and these will continue till they are resisted with either words or blows or with both. The limits of tyrants are prescribed by the endurance of those whom they oppress."

You can't build strong families with niggers who can't be insulted. We need strong African men and women who have a level of excellence and high expectations that demand to be respected. We need a people who will not allow themselves to be insulted.

Listed below are a few insulting comments and incidents that should provoke action:

- An African American woman once told me if she was walking alone down the street late at night, the last person she'd want to see is a Black man. She said she would feel more comfortable if the person was a Black woman, a White woman second, and a White male third.

- School administrators inform me their dropout rate is between 33 and 50 percent.

- African Americans, who are only 12 percent of the United States population, exceed Whites in penal institutions and one of every three African American males aged 18-29 were in penal institutions. America is spending $6 billion to incarcerate one million African American males.[1]

- When I walk into a store in the African American community and it is not only owned by foreigners, but they speak disrespectfully behind glass counters.

- The starting lineups at the men's NCAA or NBA finals consists of all brothers, but the coaches, management, and audience are 90 percent White.

- When I walk into a court in the Black community and the judges, lawyers, court reporters, and security guards are White, and the defendants are African American.

- Black Expo, which should be a showcase of African American businesses, yet the predominant number of businesses and sponsors are Whites.

- Our major magazines and civil rights organizations and UNCF are financed by cigarette and liquor companies and White sponsors.

- Neither of the two major political parties believe they need to develop an agenda to secure the Black vote.

- Metal detectors are being used at Black colleges because the students feel safer.

- I can't hail a taxi.

- A White male in Boston and a White female in South Carolina blamed murders they committed on Black men and everybody believed them.

- A Black male walks into a store and is monitored from the time he enters until he exits. He may have to give the store the clothes he's wearing, if he can't provide the receipt.

- Statistics show that a White male with a high school diploma has a greater chance of earning more than a Black male or Black female with a college degree.[2]

- Racist Whites use Dr. King's "I Have a Dream" speech, and take out of context being judged by the content of character, not by the color of skin, as a rationale to eliminate affirmative action.

- Non-African Americans feel they have the right to determine who can and cannot attend meetings conducted by civil rights organizations.

- Poor White communities like Little Italy in Baltimore are safer than poor adjacent African American communities.

- A city has a majority African American population, but are a minority on the police and fire departments, school board and staff, and licensed city vendors.

- When I drive through the African American community and there's construction taking place, the crews tend to be all White. Unemployed African American men stand on corners watching White men work in their neighborhoods.

- It has been said that African Americans supported Black businesses more during segregation. It has also been said that we had more businesses per capita during segregation than we have now with integration. It insults me that we have to be forced to shop with each other.

- In 1930, 20 percent of African Americans were illiterate. In 2000, the figure was 44 percent. Our illiteracy has increased, with each passing year.

- Can Black comedians tell jokes without cursing? I respect Bill Cosby and Sinbad for challenging comedians to tell jokes without using four-letter words.

- I preached in a Black church and saw White images of Jesus on the window panes, cross, books, fans, and in the minister's study. I walked into an inner-city African American school and the first thing I noticed were White president's pictures along the hallway. Maybe pastors and teachers don't realize the impact images have on African American children or maybe they do and that's why the pictures remain.

- One of my employees who had been consistently late told me I acted like the White man, because I expected him to be on time and work eight hours.

- The last time there was full employment in the African American community was during slavery.

- Many students tell me they resent being the only African American in class. On those rare occasions, when the discussion turns to African American issues, their opinions are sought as if they had been elected Black Representative of African American affairs.

- Some African Americans assume that the only way to live in an affluent neighborhood is to live in White neighborhoods. The assumption is that African Americans cannot live and maintain an affluent neighborhood by themselves.

- The only institutions that make it in the African American community are churches, barbecue shops that sell pork, and other fast food joints and franchises, liquor stores, barber shops, beauty shops, funeral homes, and vendors who only sell T-shirts and incense. Is this the state of the Black economy?

- A teacher once said about a child, "She's pretty, and she's Black." Lying deep in her statement is the assumption that pretty and black are diametrically opposed to each other. She was surprised the little girl could be both.

- A young lady who was the offspring of an African American father and a White mother declared on national television that she wanted to be classified as White. She told her father she wished he had never existed.

- Have you ever sat in traffic court? You may live in a city with a majority White population, but a day in traffic court will have you believing that the city is all African American. Don't Whites speed and violate traffic laws?

- Have you ever seen Christian guards patrolling the mosque? No, but I've seen Muslim guards patrol the church.

- Black rappers are encouraged and allowed to call African American women "B's," but when Michael Jackson makes a derogatory inference about Jewish culture, he is forced to recall his song and to have it redone.

- It was insulting to the million plus African American men in Washington on October the 16th to be told we were only 400,000. Was that based on 3/5 of a person?

What will it take to insult us? How large must the insult be to inspire us, to move from theory to practice? What will it take to say, "I'm sick and tired of being sick and tired?" What will it take to save the Black family? How high does the divorce rate have to grow before we take action? How many African American males have to be incarcerated for us to respond? How many African American girls have to become pregnant before we make a change? How many African American children have to live in single-parent homes before the village becomes involved?

The next chapter is the culmination of all my ideas on how to restore the Black family.

CHAPTER TEN

RESTORING THE VILLAGE

*When the festival was over, they started back home.
But the boy Jesus stayed in Jerusalem. His
parents did not know this. They thought
that he was with the group. So they
traveled a whole day and then
started looking for him among
their relatives and friends.*
Luke 2:43-44. *Good News Translation.*

 hen a home breaks down, who in the village will rescue the children? Are there any people or institutions that have been insulted and now want to become part of the solution rather than talking about the problem?

There have been numerous studies on the African American family. No work has been more controversial than the report of Patrick Moynihan and Bill Moyers. Moynihan called the African American family matriarchal, because African American men are weak and absent and African American women are domineering.

Bill Moyers titled his report "The Vanishing Black Family." This provoked a tremendous response from African American scholars, including Robert Hill, Charles Willie, Andrew Billingsley, Wade Nobles, Harriet McAdoo, K. Sue Jewelle, Reginald Clark, and Nathan and Julia Hare, who felt the slant was too negative and did not articulate the strengths.

Thirty years after Moynihan and Moyers, the African American family remains in trouble. The weaknesses have been exacerbated, but the strengths remain. Over the past 30 years, there have been numerous books and thousands of seminars and conferences, but no one has been able to answer the central question: When the home breaks down, when the father is absent, when the mother is addicted, when the family suffers from poverty, drugs, and crime, which individual or institution can come to the rescue of the children?

Who is available? Many middle-class families with both parents present are having difficulties paying bills, staying together and raising children. Will this group find the time, money, and interest to save our children? Will African American public school teachers save our children? Can they save our children while sending their children to private schools? Do you think they would teach with more fervor if their biological children were in their schools? I don't think a teacher would pass their child because of social promotion.

I used to believe Du Bois's talented tenth theory, i.e., that the solutions to our problems lie in the hands of the middle class. Unfortunately, many members of this class make decisions in the best interest of their children, not for the masses.

I now believe the salvation of the African American family lies in the hands of the village. The village is made up of under, lower, middle, and upper classes, males and females, those with elementary and high school diplomas, undergraduate and graduate degrees. It consists of unemployed, underemployed, employed, and entrepreneurs. Like Nehemiah, African

Americans living in one neighborhood, but returning home and rebuilding walls. There is only one criterion to be a member of the village. You must have a collective value system and believe *I am because we are*.

Author Shelby Steele said he resents being asked to be a role model.[1] Like Clarence Thomas he believes that "I got mine and you have yours to get." I've engaged many so-called conservatives in dialog on this subject. Many of them say it's enough to simply work, raise children, pay taxes, maintain property, help children with homework, and take the family to church. They believe that since they're not on welfare, they're doing enough.

I try to understand their analysis. It is true, one of the most revolutionary things you can do is to keep your marriage intact and raise your children. I believe that is the *minimum*. Sometimes it's more revolutionary to miss a meeting, go home and help your children with their homework or take your wife out to dinner. My wife, Rita, talked to a woman who said she and her husband hadn't gone out on a date in three years. They had two beautiful children, and he was actively involved in rites of passage and mentoring programs. Unfortunately, he had gone to the other extreme. He was trying to father all the children Shelby Steele and Clarence Thomas had disowned, but unfortunately, was ignoring his own family. In the spirit of Maat we need to find balance between Shelby Steele and Mr. Revolutionary.

The million-dollar question remains - when the home breaks down, who or what institution will rescue our children? The African proverb, it takes a whole village to raise a child, has risen in popularity over the past

145

three decades. It's now used as the title for seminars and conferences. Everyone talks about the good old days when elders in the neighborhood gave direction and discipline to youth. We like talking about the good old days, and for many of us, that's all it is, just talk. If we really valued those good old days, we would be doing everything possible to implement them, or something better.

All of us have good-old-days stories in which someone from the village saved us. Let me share mine. I was 14 and a freshman in high school. This particular afternoon, the school was having a teacher in-service. All students were dismissed at noon. I conveniently decided not to tell my parents of this schedule change, because I had made plans earlier that week for my girlfriend and me to visit my house where we were going to express ourselves sexually. We were walking up the stairs when my neighbor, Mrs. Nolan, poked her head out the window and said, "You're home awfully early, Jerome." And I said, "yes ma'am, Kathy and I were going to sit on the porch and review our algebra problems from this morning." She then said, "Does your mother know you're home this early and do you want me to call her?" I said, "No ma'am, I'll go inside and call her while Kathy sits on the porch." Mrs. Nolan saved my career that day. If Kathy had become pregnant, she might not have been the doctor she is today. If I had impregnated her my father would have held me accountable. My father had a mutual fund for me that was to be used either for college or to start a business. My father had warned me if I made a baby all the money would go to the child. Thank you, Mrs. Nolan.

High school students have too much discretionary time. Another member from my village, Gerald Richards, became my track coach. He'd have us running from 3:00 to 6:00 p.m. every day until we were exhausted. At 6:00 he would say, "Now the workout will begin." He said "anybody can run when they're fresh. What I need to know is, can you run when you are tired?" I didn't have time to get in trouble or learn to quit, thanks to Gerald Richards.

Many of us talk about those good old days, but how many of us have the names, addresses, and telephone numbers of five neighbors? When was the last time you visited your neighbors or invited them over?

Our parents knew they could not raise their children by themselves. Children don't belong to parents, they belong to the village. Our parents did not work downtown, come home, lock the door, and watch television the remainder of the evening. Our parents sat on the porch, walked down the block, and talked to Mrs. Nolan and Mr. Richards. The more they talked, the better they knew them. And the more they trusted them with disciplining their children.

Can you trust someone you don't know? Can you know someone you don't talk to? Can you talk to someone you don't see - except by telephone? Why is it that we don't sit on the porch anymore? Why don't we walk down the block? Why is it that many of us feel we don't have enough time? We have microwaves, TV dinners, fast-food franchises, dishwashers, unlike our parents and grandparents who had to do most things by hand and from scratch.

One reason why the village broke down is that we no longer find time to talk with our neighbors. Granted, it is very difficult, if not impossible, to sit out on the porch between November and March in colder climates, but past generations after northern migrations found ways. The village is potentially stronger in warmer parts of the country, where they have a greater opportunity to interact with one another. Another factor could be changing housing patterns. More of us used to live in single-family dwellings; some were viewed as shacks. When we migrated north, we went vertical. Housing developments in urban centers were designed for rats not people. Concentrated poverty eliminates positive role models.

Two major hindrances to family and village development are television and the declining time adults spend with children. The family and village were more cohesive when parents spent more time with their children. The family and village becomes less cohesive and influential when adults spend eight hours or more working away from their family.

The other hindrance to village development and parental influence is television, which did not exist until the 1950's. Many of us, including myself, from time to time would rather be inside the house, watching our favorite TV show, than sitting on the porch, walking down the block, and talking to neighbors. If a parent does not arrive home until 6:00 or 7:00 p.m., then has to make dinner and desires to watch a favorite television show, where is the time to walk down the block? I recommend all families play the game 1910, once a week. Imagine living without television for a day. Let's reactivate the village by turning the television off. Tape your favorite show, *if* we want to return to the good old days.

The formula our parents and grandparents used to raise us was: the Lord, the village, common sense, the belt, and a home-cooked meal. The current formula is: BET, a BA degree, a BMW, Burger King, and being buddies with your children. Our parents and grandparents might not have had college degrees, but they had common sense. They didn't try to reason with their children when they threw plates across a restaurant. They whipped their children in public and the child didn't dare think about calling the state. They knew their children would grow strong and healthy off greens, "pot liquor," and cornbread, not a "Happy Meal" from McDonald's.

We might think living in America is better with 60+ channels to choose from versus living in the rural part of Ghana where people literally go to bed when the sun goes down; but after 25,000 sexual and violent acts, you need to rethink that position.

Many people say in the good old days, people had the same values. Most families knew the Ten Commandments and had reverence for the Lord. That's why they could entrust their children to other adults. It would be foolish and naive to entrust your children to neighbors who may be involved in drug trafficking, sexual molestation, gang involvement and other immoral activities. People without values are dangerous. People without values are unpredictable. People without values cannot be trusted.

Our elders used to say to a child on the block,

"You're Mrs. Jones's girl, or you're Mr. Brown's boy." That laid the foundation and provided the context for the discussion. When elders associated you with a family, they knew your values. They could predict your behavior because they knew your parents and grandparents. Children knew the elder was establishing the family lineage, accountability, and respect. You were more than Jerome or Kathy. You were the Browns' boy and the Joneses' girl; and when an elder asked you a question, you had to answer. If not, you knew that the elder would talk to your parents or grandparents.

Back then, adults were secure and mature. They encouraged other adults to take an active role in their child's growth and development. Parents and neighbors were on the same side. Teachers and parents were also on the same side. They created a village for each other. Today, we have parents who will curse out teachers and neighbors and get their side of the story later. Elders are afraid to speak, much less chastise children. They are not confident they will receive support from parents and respect from children.

There has been much discussion in America about how immigrants, including Africans from the continent and the Caribbean, have performed better educationally and economically than groups who have been here longer. This is comparing immigrants to slaves. It is unfair to compare someone who voluntarily came here with their culture intact to a person who was forced to come here and their culture, family, and friends have been denied them. Studies indicate immigrants, including African Americans who travel elsewhere, have a higher educational attainment, capital, possess a higher level of self-esteem, and would be successful anywhere.[2]

Cultural unity can overcome racism. A group that knows its culture can pool resources together to start businesses. They can study together and perform better on achievement tests. They can employ other group members, organize the village, patrol their neighborhoods, and keep them safe. African Americans must use their culture to restore the village. One of our strengths is the extended family.

Research shows that 90 percent of African American children who were born out of wedlock are reared in an extended family.[3] I am pleased that so many African Americans are taking their caretaker roles seriously. Many adults are reaching back to less fortunate family members to give them a sense of direction.

Foreign entrepreneurs in the African American community have learned not to depend on the government for capital, but on family. Extended family members live together in order to save mortgage and rent payments to create capital to start or build their business. I've been challenged on my position that my sons need to leave home on their 18th birthday and preferably go to college. I want them to become self-sufficient. We have too many children, especially African American males 18 years and older, still living at home with their parents, becoming more and more irresponsible.

The extended family should not produce weak and irresponsible people. Relatives should pay rent, work, and save toward the agreed-upon goal, whether it is self-sufficiency or the capitalization of a family business. I am appalled by the number of young adult males who are still living with their mothers - unemployed and not in school. They have the nerve to get annoyed when mothers ask them to carry the groceries upstairs, the same groceries that they'll be consuming.

The Black family is more than father-mother-sister-brother. Earlier we used the term "augmented families," which includes nonrelated members. There are an estimated 850,000 augmented families that constitute 8 percent of Black households.[4]

There are numerous unsung heroes in the African American community who have taken in not only nieces, nephews, and cousins, but also people from the community. Seldom does the media share their stories. People often ask, "What can I do?" I remind them of some tremendous individuals who took that question and developed institutions.

The Amos family is a successful Black family. Kent Amos is a successful business executive, and Carmen, his wife is also gainfully employed. They have two children. Unlike some of the teachers in their community who sent their children to private schools, they decided to send their children to the public school in the neighborhood in which they resided. They soon realized that they had put their own children at risk of being socialized by the neighborhood children. So Kent and Carmen decided that they would have to socialize not only their biological children but the larger community as well. They told their children to invite their friends over during the evening. There wasn't much to do anyway, so the children responded positively.

I'm sure Kent and Carmen did not know then how

great the response would be. What started out as an evening activity for a couple of children eventually attracted some 50 children! Kent and Carmen took them everywhere they took their children, including vacations. All the children were involved in cleaning the house, making dinner, and washing dishes.

As the numbers began to swell, they moved their program to the local neighborhood school. After nearly ten years, Kent and Carmen report that of the fifty members of this augmented family, 18 had graduated from college and another 18 were still in college, others were employed. Only a few had been lost to the streets.

Oprah Winfrey has decided that she will adopt 100 families, but before she gives them money for housing, education, and other economic resources they will need, they are required to receive training in values to break the poverty mentality. Through the assistance of a local social service agency, one hundred families are being screened and provided classes. Then and only then will she empower them economically.

Joseph Marshall and Reverend Cecil Williams in San Francisco are doing excellent work to restore the village. Joseph Marshall has developed the Omega Boys Club which has rescued more than 500 African American youth from the streets and sent 108 of them to college. They succeeded because they meet the boys on the streets, and provide mentorship, guidance, and counseling.

Reverend Cecil Williams of the Glide Memorial Church in San Francisco also decided the church needs to meet its members on the street and bring them into the house of the Lord. He has successfully demonstrated to many of the indigent that Christ is greater than crack, the Holy Spirit is greater than heroin, and the Lord is greater than liquor. Reverend Williams has seen over the past 30 years how drugs have become the new form of slavery. He realized that many people had made drugs their god, so he reversed their thinking.

Reverend Craig Sorres in Atlanta and the Program Victory House have helped more than 9,000 homeless African American and Latino males to become self-sufficient. Reverend Sorres employs a holistic three-step approach called S.E.E. (Spiritual, Emotional, Economic). Participants in the program are involved in public worship, other church-related activities, individual and group counseling, and job training and placement. Sorres is a living example of what he preaches. He lives, works, and ministers in the same community.

The Hale House in New York is another illustration of what individuals can do to make a difference. More than three decades ago, the late Mrs. Hale realized that drug addiction was destroying infants and adults. She took thousands of drug-addicted babies who had been abandoned or neglected by their mothers. She nurtured and gave them love. She provided a nutritious diet and an environment which allowed them to thrive and heal.

When the home breaks down, our first line of defense should be the extended and augmented family. The second institution that we should look to is the school. Some people might argue that the church or community organization is the logical second rescue level and I appreciate their position. However, my choice is based on the 1950 study conducted by the University of Michigan that found that home, school, and church were the three major influences upon our children, respectively. Today, the three major influences are the peer group, rap music, and the media. Interestingly, schools ranked number two before Brown vs. the Topeka Board of Education and integration. The 1950's school was led by an African American principal and teachers, who lived in the neighborhood, attended the local church, and had a vested interest in their children's growth and development. Today's school is populated by teachers of different races, who no longer live in the community, nor do they have a vested interest in the children they teach. In many neighborhoods, the school has become a hostile institution where parents are not welcomed to visit their children's classrooms. If parents had bad experiences as students there, it might be even more difficult attracting them to a PTA meeting.

Since our children spend more time in school than in any other institution, schools need to be an integral part of the village. It is my desire to return schools to their pre-1954 vantage position. Fortunately, a few village schools exist today. The Council of Independent Black Institutions (CIBI) boasts over 50 Africentric academically sound schools nationwide. Other schools are modeled upon the research of James Comer and the late Ron Edmonds. They have formed a marriage between community, school, and social service agencies. African American immersion schools are stellar examples.

These schools realize that when homes break down,

children will need more from schools, not less. I am amazed at teachers who are critical of what parents are not doing, and then give lower expectations and less time on task. If they accept their own logic, if the home has failed, shouldn't that require more from educators?

I have seen strong principals create a village out of their school with afterschool programs including tutorial, cultural, and recreational activities. These programs not only develop children, but they keep them safe and away from gangs and drugs. Many schools nationwide are conducting rites of passage programs, debates, spelling bees, math contests, and science fairs.

The third line of defense after extended and augmented families and schools is the church. There are more than 75,000 Black churches that receive annual contributions in excess of $2 billion and assets of more than $50 billion.[5] Approximately 13 million African Americans attend church if we extrapolate 40 percent attendance from 32 million African Americans.

There are basically three types of churches: entertainment, containment, and liberation. In entertainment churches, members are very emotional, they sing, holler, and shout, but they do very little work. Containment churches are only open on Sunday from 11:00 a.m. to 1:00 p.m. Liberation churches are driven by a theology, which requires us to feed the hungry, clothe the naked, and set the captives free. Liberation churches serve a greater percentage of men and young people than entertainment and containment churches, because they have more relevant programs and ministries open every day of the week. We Christians say our children are our future, but most churches allocate very little space, money, and time on the youth worship service. How many churches allow youth to sleep over while providing religious, cultural, and recreational activities? How many adults are willing to volunteer a weekend to empower our youth?

Much has been said about the tremendous work of the Nation of Islam at empowering our people, but there is no comparison between the mosque and the church on who has fed, clothed, and housed the needy. It is unfair to compare the Nation of Islam to entertainment and containment churches. In almost every city liberation churches are helping to stimulate the Black economy by buying properties, developing low-income housing, and opening restaurants, bakeries, bookstores, clothing stores, and banquet halls. We need more churches to develop employment ministries that would provide counseling, technical assistance, and computer training. We need churches that will teach entrepreneurship and develop strategies for capital acquisition.

The Shrine of the Black Madonna owns three of the best African American bookstores in the country. They have farmland in Georgia called Beulahland. They provide housing for many of their members. When I was their guest speaker in Detroit and Atlanta, I didn't stay at the Hyatt, Hilton, or the Marriott, I stayed in their housing complex.

Shrine members have gone beyond just talking about the village. In one housing complex I visited, I saw children working on computers and other educational and recreational equipment under the supervision of den mothers, while their parents lived on another floor.

This lifestyle would not be palatable for most of us who are locked into the nuclear family concept. Ironically, these opponents of the Shrine's living arrangements readily send their children to boarding schools operated by Europeans.

The last line of defense we have when the home breaks down is community organizations. Kwame Toure (Stokely Carmichael) consistently reminded us that we all need to become active in an organization. Our communities are weak because we are not organized. Many African Americans who think like Shelby Steele and Clarence Thomas don't feel it's their responsibility to volunteer and empower those less fortunate.

All children need a safety net. My safety net was provided by neighbors, a track coach, and local business owners who employed me after school, weekends and summers. The White community has a stronger safety net for their children. One day a White boy name Joey threw a rock in a cleaners' window. Later that evening, he was visited by three White male owners and was told he was responsible for the broken window which cost $250. They also told him he would be able to pay for it because he now had a part-time job in the cleaners. The first monies would pay for the window, and deductions would be made from subsequent checks to open a mutual fund for college. They would monitor his progress monthly.

Across town in the African American community, Willie also breaks a window. The reality is that the window will probably not be owned by African Americans, but by foreigners who would not be as generous as the White owners. The broken window does not provide a job, learning experience, mutual fund, college tuition, but prosecution or a bullet. We need an African American village that would provide a safety net for our children. This would require African American adults to start businesses and mentor our children. We have a generation of youth who have never worked or seen someone in their family or building work. The safety net can break the cycle of poverty.

Why are there more foreign-owned businesses in the Black community than African American? Why are they more profitable? Did they receive a low interest loan? Did Africans from the Caribbean, who per capita also own more businesses than African Americans, also receive a low interest loan? In my book, *Black Economics: Solutions for Economic and Community Empowerment,* I describe cultural models to raise capital called susu and Ujamaa. People who trust each other are able to pool their resources together to become entrepreneurs. We could restore the village with Ujamaa, which would reduce our unemployment rate and create a safety net for our youth.[6]

We need African American organizations to teach our children their history and culture. The Jewish community does not expect public schools to teach their children about Yom Kippur. Rites of passage programs must be an integral component of the village, and they must be strong enough to compete with gangs. The village must redefine for our youth the definition of manhood and womanhood. Presently, there are more than 300 rites of passage programs nationwide. Ten minimal standards have been agreed upon. Each child will learn spirituality, Africentricity, economics, politics, career development, sexual education, physical development, family responsibility, values, and community involvement.

Rites of passage programs should be taken seriously. They cannot be implemented with a three-month summer grant. The word "rites" is plural and continuous. The program should be designed so boys and girls move from one developmental stage to another. Rites of passage programs require a long-term commitment from both adults and youth. A twelve-year-old boy should not receive a manhood ceremony after only a few months.

The last village program that I think is essential is a crime watch group. I reserved this for last because it requires a great degree of seriousness. Today KKK means Kids Killing Kids. Many of our youth are armed, dangerous, and committed to protecting their turf. I believe the only way to take back our streets and our children is for God-fearing, humble, and consistent African American men to patrol the streets. We need men to commit time, energy, and resources to maintain the safety of our communities.

Of all the things I've done in my life, one of the most rewarding and challenging has been the implementation of our crime watch group, Community of Men. We walk the streets, pass out literature, and talk to brothers about the importation of guns and drugs into our community. We offer them economic alternatives to dealing drugs, tutorial support, cultural and recreational activities, and a meal.

When we first met to talk about the problem, 175 men were in attendance. When we marched we had 68, but when we hit the streets we dropped to 20. I'm reminded of Gideon who started with 32,000 and ended with 300. I challenge all African American men who were in Washington to join an organization and consistently work to achieve their goals.

We also need a village for our marriages. Spouses need other couples when they're experiencing problems. I often ask spouses how frequently they interact with couples. When you're experiencing problems, the last people you need to interact with are those who are unhappily married, divorced or who have never been married. It is imperative that you develop a village of happy married couples who believe in God and can encourage you to perservere. It really disappoints me when a husband or wife tell me they are no longer married. They asked me to attend the wedding, but they give me no opportunity to help in reconciliation. If we sought the resources of the village, we could reduce our divorce rate.

In conclusion, the future of the Black family lies in the hands of the village. White America has spoken via the public and private sector that help is not forthcoming. We must return to God, start businesses, and reclaim our youth.

The following chapter is actually an appendage for White professionals working with African American families. While they are often viewed as experts on the Black family, many of them have never lived in the African American community or taken one course in Africentricity.

We must restore the village to save the family.

CHAPTER ELEVEN

CULTURAL MYTHS

Jesus I know and Paul I know. But who are you?
Acts 19:15. *New King James Version*

 ne third of my workshops are given to teachers, social workers, psychologists and other related professionals who interact with African American families. The White component of that audience has been increasing over the years for a variety of reasons, which include African Americans having greater options to choose from, lack of interest in education and social services, income and the failure to pass the entrance exam. I stated earlier that the future of African American children, specifically African American boys, lies in the hands of White female teachers.

This last chapter is designed to equip White professionals who have never lived in the African American community or taken any courses on African American history and culture to understand the culture of the children they are teaching. These people have been given the authority to label and categorize our families and ultimately determine our destiny. Sometimes, I get the feeling that many Whites are looking for a pill that will enable them to understand the African American family. Some Whites who are paid to educate and service African American children don't listen to my presentation, sit in the rear of the auditorium, talk with their peers, or read the newspaper. During the question-and-answer period, I try to engage Whites in the discussion, because they have our children; therefore we need to know their thoughts, views, and values. I find it significant that a greater percentage of African Americans purchase the materials than White professionals. If Whites do express an interest, most request their institution to buy the materials. In contrast, African Americans tend to purchase the materials from their own resources.

The theoretical paradigm I'm presenting here will help White professionals understand the African American family. It is as follows:

Teacher/Professional   1) Admit   Student/Client
                                    2) understand
                                    3) appreciate

The first step is to *admit* that race, culture, and ethnicity are factors to be considered in teaching or providing services. Many White professionals are not willing to admit this. They tell me, "I see children as children, people are people. We are all the same in God's eye. We need to quit looking for differences and look for similarities." The favorite phrase is "can't we all just get along?" This response has provoked me to create another category that I call Level 0: *Denial.* Coincidentally, the people that deny race, culture, and ethnicity see race-related issues better than anyone else.

I met one of these "liberal" teachers on one of my speaking engagements. She said she didn't see color. She saw children as children. I asked Ms. Liberal if I could visit her classroom after my presentation. The ethnic breakdown of her students was 85 percent African American and Latino population and 15 percent

White. Her bulletin board had White images and 90 percent of the books in the library were about, for, and written by Whites. For someone so colorblind, she sure was fixated on one color. She was in a classic state of denial.

It is very difficult, if not impossible for me to work with professionals who are in this mental state. Not only do they deny that race, culture, and ethnicity should be considered, but they simultaneously blame the victims for their ineffectiveness. Many teachers in denial are quick to blame socio-demographics and genetics. How can people who see people as people know so much about poverty, single parenting, and melanin's relationship to intelligence?

The second step in understanding the Black family is to *understand* the culture. Immerse yourself in the literature and the neighborhood. If you're going to work with Black people it's only common sense that you know your clientele. They've had very little interaction and taken sparse if not any culture-related courses in college.

Research by Peters and Bennett has uncovered the following ten major myths about the Black family.

1. Raw and uncontrolled sex, according to the biggest and most pervasive myth, is at the root of the Black family problem.
2. The root cause of the problem, according to the second most widely disseminated myth, is loose morals.
3. Blacks lack a family tradition and came to America without a sense of morality and a background of stable sexual relationships.

4. The bonds of the Black family were destroyed in slavery.
5. The Black family collapsed after Emancipation.
6. The Black family collapsed after the Great Migration to the North.
7. The Black family is a product of White paternalism and government welfare.
8. The Black family has always been a matriarchy characterized by strong and domineering women and weak and absent men.
9. Black men cannot sustain stable relationships.
10. The history of the Black family is a history of fussing and fighting by hard-hearted men and heartless women.[1]

Professionals label our children without any prior knowledge of multicultural nomenclature. Listed below are multicultural terms that I would like you to define.

Racism	Overt racism
Institutional racism	White Supremacy
Sexism	Classism
Prejudice	Integration
Desegregation	Monolithic
Stereotypes	Xenophilic
Xenophobic	Non-White minority majority
Centricity	Africentricity
Eurocentricity	Multiculturalism
Diversity	Melting-pot theory
Salad-bowl theory	Culturally deprived
Inclusion	History
Contribution history	Negro history

African history	Chattel slavery
Indentured servitude	Matrilineal
Matriarch	Third World
First World	Slave
Enslaved African	Upper and Lower Egypt
Continent	At-risk youth
At-risk institutions	Standard English
Black English	Racial psychopaths
Menticide	Mystery system
Classics	Hyperactive
Holidays	Holy Days
Entertainment	Innerattainment
Equity	Good hair
Pretty Eyes	Black
White	Melanin
Reparations	

As you're able to define these terms from an Africentric perspective, you'll better understand African American history and culture. I encourage you to read the work of Cheikh Anta Diop, Molefi Asante, Frances Welsing, Bobby Wright, Marimba Ani, and Oba T'Shaka. If more White professionals and "Black Anglo-Saxons" read these authors with an open mind and not in a state of denial, we could eradicate or reduce the impact of White supremacy.

The last and most important step to understanding the Black family is to *appreciate* the culture. If it's possible for "Black Anglo-Saxons" to not want to be African, then it's not so surprising that Whites might not want to deal with the culture either. Many "Black Anglo-Saxons" and White professionals dislike the way African American males walk, talk, shrug their shoulders, and stare at them. What they fail to appreciate is that the African American male is as proud as a peacock, strong as Shaka, intelligent as Imhotep, perservering as Mandela, graceful as Michael Jordan, visionary as Martin Luther King, bold as Malcolm X, and precise as Ben Carson.

I often show professionals pictures of African American males and ask them, "Do you see a doctor or a drug dealer? A criminal or a computer programmer?" I believe that what you see *in* the child will be what you try to produce *out* of the child.

In the ideal world, both the professional and the client would function at level three. They would admit, understand, and appreciate the culture. More than anyone, professionals should be the leaders in cultural sensitivity. In many situations between teacher and student, social worker and client, it is the student and client who are more culturally grounded in Africentricity than the professional. This creates cultural incongruence and makes success problematic. To effectively work with African American families, there must be an appreciation of the culture. Optimally, the teacher and student will appreciate the culture, creating cultural congruence which is essential for success.

Unfortunately, what I see in the educational and social service sector is not education and empowerment, but professionals who label, categorize, and control. The labels and categories include: remedial reading classes, lower-track classes, regular classes, honors, advanced placement, magnet schools, gifted and talented programs, behavior disordered, educationally and mentally handicapped, mentally retarded, learning disabled, hyperactive, and attention deficit disorder.

Professionals who are left-brain thinkers, tend to label, categorize, compartmentalize, and separate the whole into various parts. People who are insecure equate different with deficient, are obsessed with power, which is why they must label, define, categorize, and control.

The following table shows the destructive power of labeling African Americans.

Students

African American	European (White American)
Drug addict	Chemically dependent/substance abuser
Broken home	Solo-parenting
Aggressive	Assertive, Good leadership potential
Mentally retarded	Underachiever
Truant	Bored, suffering from school phobia
Hyperactive	High energy level
Lazy	Meditating, in deep thought
Gangs	Good White boys having fun

ATHLETES

African American	European (White American)
Raw talent	Heady
Animal	Sound fundamentals
Burner	Worker
Brute	Project (White owner's pet)
Hot dog	Team player

Words reflect people's values, and you can't separate one from the other. In the list of multicultural terms, the words black and white were provided. If you look in a Thesaurus, there are more than 265 negative connotations to the word "black," like dark and evil. There's blackball, black list, a dark Monday, the dark continent and black funerals. The word "white" is associated with purity, angels, weddings, and little white lies. "We can't all get along," until we become more sensitive and accurate on words and labels usage. More importantly, we have to ask ourselves the truth about our intentions when we label and categorize children and families.

I don't believe anyone was born racist. Racism is not transmitted through the genes. Racism did not originate with parents. After all, who - or what - taught them to hate? Racism is transmitted through the media and curriculum which shape our worldview.

As Joyce Ladner explains in *Death of White Sociology*, traditionally sociological studies of the African American family have been divided into four categories:

1) Only poor families were studied.
2) The Black middle class was ignored.
3) The victim was blamed.
4) Black families were ignored.[2]

I would like for you to monitor a week's worth of newspapers in your city. Cut out the articles about African American people and then categorize them at the end of the week. We did this recently with the *New York Times*. Of the 25 articles that were written about African American people, 20 of them involved crime, and five were poverty related. There were no articles about African American achievement that week.

It would be very difficult for the average White person or White professional to have a broad and accurate perspective of African American families with a media that distorts reality. The same also applies in the curriculum. One of the major reasons why racism flourishes is because school curricula are founded and grounded in White supremacy. Many African American children hate themselves and associate being smart with being White because they're only given 28 days minus weekends to learn their history and culture.

Let's take a quiz on inclusion. In the left column below is the White contributor to history. Your responsibility is to include a Black contributor from that same timeframe.

INCLUSION

European (White) American	African American
Abraham Lincoln	
Thomas Edison	
Alexander Bell	
Hippocrates	
Napoleon	
The Roman Army	
Greece	
Franklin Delano Roosevelt	
John F. Kennedy	

The racial polarization throughout the O.J. Simpson case and after the verdict reinforced the Kerner Commission report of 1968 and repeated 25 years later in the excellent book *Two Nations* by Andrew Hackman. Johnny Cochran did not introduce racism in his closing argument; racism existed at the very outset of the case with the Los Angeles Police Department.

The O.J. Simpson case did not create two nations. White supremacy is the culprit and we will never "just get along" until it is abolished. Some Whites still believe Rodney King was resisting arrest when he was moving while being beat 56 times. At the Million Man March, some people believed the media's lie that 400,000 African American men were being led by a hate monger. Others saw more than a million African American men hear a God-fearing man speak on atonement, reconciliation, and responsibility. The Park Service assumed from a White perspective that in a nine-square-foot area, there would only be three persons. The actual pictures showed six brothers in a nine-square-foot area. From an African perspective, space is viewed differently. This is also evident at an African American party. We enjoy it more when we are closer to each other.

Let's take another quiz on three controversial issues: poverty, drugs, and crime. There are 36 million people in America who live below the poverty level. They are divided into two groups: group one has is 11 million people and group two has 25 million. One group is White and the other group is Black and Latino. Which group would you assign which number? The correct answer is that 25 million Whites and 11 million Blacks and Latinos live below the poverty line.[3]

The total hard drug (cocaine or heroin) users in America, can be divided into two groups: group one is 76 percent and group two is 24 percent. One group is

Black and Latino and the other group is White. Which group has which percentage? The correct answer is that 76 percent of all hard drug users are White and 24 percent are Black and Latino.[4] What percentage of crime is white collar? The correct answer is that 80 percent of the crime in America is white collar crime and 20 percent of the crime in America involves handguns and/or knives.[5] The majority of crimes are embezzlement and fraud, not homicide and armed robbery. An unemployed African American father steals a television set and receives a sentence of six years. A White male stockbroker embezzles $2 million and receives a $5,500 fine. The term capital punishment is accurate - if you have capital, you don't get punished!

What percentage of African American families earn more than $35,000 (middle class)? What percentage earn between $15,000 and $35,000 (working class)? What percentage earn less than $15,000? The correct answers are 30 percent of African American families earn more than $35,000. *The Cosby Show* is real. Thirty-two percent of African American families earn between $15,000 and $35,000. The show *Roc* is also true. Thirty-eight percent of African American families live below the poverty line.[6] The show *Good Times* is real also. The original *Good Times* included a father and mother before racist producers decided that the Black family didn't need a strong father and mother and could be led by a fool named J.J.

I'm amazed when White social workers discuss the Black family in a monolithic and homogeneous fashion. Which African American family are you describing? *Cosby, Roc,* or *Good Times*? Extended, nuclear, augmented, or single? Advanced degrees or illiterate? Families who believe in Jesus, Allah, Yahweh, Buddha, Maat, Nguzo Saba, New Jack, or Hip Hop? There are many educators who were only taught to teach the *Leave it To Beaver* type children. Presently, we need professionals to work with Murphy Brown's child and Bebe kids.

Racists often say African Americans are culturally deprived. Everyone has a culture. People that like to define, label, and categorize assume that if you don't possess their culture you're deprived. This reminds me of the Standard English debate. Which English is correct? That spoken in London? Ted Kennedy's English spoken in Boston, Jimmy Carter's English spoken in Georgia, or Ronald Reagan's English spoken in California? In London they laugh at American English. Which English is correct?

Most Whites assume that African people lost their culture in the Middle Passage. The excellent research and writings of Wade Nobles, Asa Hilliard, Molefi Asante, and Melville Herskovits document the fact that African culture survived the dungeons, slave ships, plantations, and mass migrations. Listed below are brief illustrations of African cultural expressions.

African American Culture

Worldview - Harmony, nature, xenophilic, pro life
History - 3.75 million years old, Garden of Eden
    flows through the Nile
Religion - belief in monotheism and life after death
Values - Maat, Ten Commandments, Nguzo Saba
Family - extended, augmented

Clothes - bright, gele, dashiki, loppa
Hair - braids, dreadlocks, natural
Food - Curry or jerk chicken, okra, watermelon, mango, millet
Flag - red, black, and green
Allegiance - Here's to this flag of mine
Anthem - Lift Every Voice and Sing
Language - Swahili, Ebonics
Music - gospel, soul, jazz, blues, rap
Holy Days - January 15 and the Third Monday in January (Martin Luther King's birthday); February (Black Liberation month); May 19 (Malcolm X's birthday); June 19 (June Teenth celebration); August 17 (Marcus Garvey's birthday); October 16 (Day of Atonement); December 26 to January 1 (Kwanzaa).
Innerattainment - call and chant, drummers, dancers and audience are one

The great religious philosopher John Mbiti elaborates on African culture this way: "I am because we are."[7] In African culture *we* is more important than *I*. The group is more important than the individual. The identity and existence of an individual is contingent upon the larger group. My scoring 30 points in a basketball game and breaking a school record is insignificant if our team loses.

The terms "brother" and "sister" are part of an African philosophy of "fictive kinship." As African people, we are all members of the same family. When Whites hear Africans use "brother" or "sister," they believe we're speaking literally. At an integrated party, an African was asked what he did for a living. He said he was a

Christian and he worships and praises his Lord and Savior Jesus Christ. The people asking the question grew irritated because they were trying to find out what type of work he did. They finally asked him how do you earn income? He said he worked as an engineer, but that's not who I am. Too many of us have allowed ourselves to be defined by what we do for a living, which is why, unfortunately, many of us suffer an identity crisis when we become unemployed.

In the excellent book, *Black and White Styles in Conflict*, Thomas Kochman describes some of the differences between the two cultures that White professionals need to appreciate.[8] One is tone of expression. If an issue is being discussed between Blacks and Whites, oftentimes Whites are reserved, unemotional, and detached from the conversation while African Americans are more intense and emotional. Many White professionals are uncomfortable with such displays of passion, believing that violence could erupt.

Another illustration of conflicting styles is the relationship between the speaker and audience or teacher and students. Many Whites feel they should be absolutely quiet during a lecture. On the other hand, African Americans tend to talk and make comments in the spirit of call and chant response. Tony Brown told me of a time he was speaking to an integrated audience. The Whites were becoming irritated because the Blacks kept saying, "go Tony, go Tony. Tell them, tell them." Finally, Tony told the Whites to leave the Blacks alone because they were helping him with his speech.

In the classroom, Whites feel that students should always take turns and raise their hands before answering. Many African Americans become so involved with the discussions that, in the spirit of spontaneity, they just blurt out the answer. This is a very sensitive and complex point for the classroom teacher. I acknowledge African Americans need to be more respectful of each other, the teacher, and classroom protocol. I also have strong reservations about children being sent to the corner, principal's office, or special education for being excited about learning. As a former classroom teacher, I would much rather have 30 students eager to respond than 30 students who are so bored they fall asleep in my class. I often wonder if schools are trying to put African American children to sleep.

"Hyperactivity" is another culturally value-laden term. Hyperactivity is compared to standard normal behavior. The standard is the White child. Most African American children have greater verve and energy than White children; consequently they're considered hyperactive. I would much rather teach live, spontaneous, hyperactive children than to teach dead, bored, and unmotivated children. The real issue is not whether African American children are hyperactive, but whether the classroom teacher has provided a pedagogy and classroom environment commensurate and compatible with their energy and learning style.

Another area of conflict is that in White culture words are taken literally. In African American culture words are often used to exaggerate reality. For example, in an exciting basketball game, the winning shot was taken with one second left on the clock. African Americans will say things like "we blew them out," "we dogged them," "we killed them." To listen to them you might thing the opposing team lost by 20 points.

This also applies to the dozens, signifying, cracking, ranking, and scoring. Many White teachers hear African American children going one-on-one with each other about each other's mother. From their frame of reference, they believe a fight is eminent. The reality is those two children might be the best of friends five minutes later and the loser of the signifying contest will use his or her opponent's lines on someone else. Signifying, cracking, ranking, scoring, and the dozens are actually designed to avoid a fight.

Conflict also arise from Black and White cultures at parties. From an African perspective, the objective of a party is to have a good time by dancing, laughing, eating and drinking. African people don't use a party to network, brainstorm, or interview each other. From an African perspective, it does not matter whether you have a Ph.D. or live on AFDC. The question is, Do you want to dance?

I travel on airplanes three to four days a week. Ninety percent of the plane population are White males except on Monday, October 16, 1995, when African men took over the airlines industry. Invariably the first question White men will ask is about my career. I answer and return the question before I get a million questions about publishing and consulting and learn enough about my field to become my competitor.

From an African perspective, personal information is guarded and is shared only with people you trust. I've had some very enjoyable experiences on airplanes with Whites, mostly White women, but a few White men too. Then the conversations were not about career, materialism, or the stock market, but about family and spirituality. Words can't describe the nexus that exists when race is no longer a factor. While our cultures were not denied, our love for the Lord and family were illuminated.

Another illustration of Black and White cultural differences involves home life. African American children prefer playing with other children rather than playing by themselves or with objects. This has tremendous classroom implications because after the primary division, children are expected to work more independently and think more in the abstract and with less hands-on-artifacts. Because of their propensity toward human interaction, African American children are more influenced by their peer group and prefer working in groups. Unfortunately, African American children suffer if cooperative learning is not implemented.

I've observed the behavior of children who just received an assignment. They'll look around the room, assess the progress of their friends, and spend additional time preparing their desk before completing the project. A teacher lacking knowledge of Africentricity would punish the child for this additional loss of time. From an African perspective, the child was simply "setting the stage," which was essential for successful completion of the assignment. Setting the stage is an opportunity to prepare their environment for maximum efficiency; which includes prepar-ing themselves emotionally, cleaning their desk, and confirming that their peers are completing the assignment.

I believe it is more effective for the teacher to allow one or two extra minutes for African American children to set the stage than to punish them for the rest of the day.

A visit to an African American home can be overwhelming if one is unaccustomed to lots of people and a myriad of activities, including talking, playing, music and three televisions playing simultaneously. Social workers who define the ideal family as a father, mother, two children, and only one television on for two hours a day will be overwhelmed to see a grandmother, mother, four children, two cousins, a nephew, and a friend down the block who has been informally adopted. People who can only do one thing at a time and who must separate and categorize things would have a very difficult time appreciating the vitality of this household. Is the problem an over-stimulated home or a social worker with a vastly different approach to living?

I'm amazed when teachers try to convince me that African American children can't learn, yet if you play a rap cassette, they can memorize the words in less than five minutes. I wonder if these teachers could achieve that feat? If children can memorize Snoop, Tupac, and Dr. Dre, they can also memorize the Constitution, the 50 states and algebra and chemical formulas. The question becomes, Can an educator teach without ditto sheets and/or textbooks? Are we willing to provide lesson plans congruent with children's learning styles?

I believe two of the most significant issues involving social workers in the African American community are racial classification and adoptions. We will use a new legally created racial classification: bi-racial or multi-racial. This has significant implications for congressional districts and financial allocations. It also has cultural and social implications. Race has never been a biological term. You can't conveniently place six billion people into three neat groups, Negroid, Caucasoid, and Mongoloid. Nor can you explain how Noah's three sons, Ham, Shem, and Japheth, each represented three distinct races! The theory was born in America, that "one drop of Black blood makes you Black." Whites were in the majority in America; they didn't feel the need to increase their numbers with "half-breeds." In Central and South America where Whites were a minority, they reversed the criterion, i.e., one drop of White blood classified you as White.

As we enter the 21st century, people of color will constitute 50 percent of the workforce.[9] Whites will then become the minority. One of the greatest fears of a White supremacist is genetic annihilation.

Our struggle over identity began when we were taken from Africa. Originally we were Africans, but we were told to call ourselves colored, Negro, Black, and Afro American. Presently, we call ourselves African Americans, even though two-thirds of our population prefer using the term Black. We have almost completed the circle and are one word away from what we called ourselves 400 years ago.

Within this context, we have an estimated 800,000 African Americans passing for White.[10] Now we have the additional baggage of a group of people calling themselves bi-racial. For that matter, what American does not have a mixture from some other race? Not only will this bi-racial classification affect us politically and economically, but more importantly, psychologically. It is understandable in a country based on White supremacy why some people would rather be White or bi-racial. I wonder though, when these people are stopped by the police to receive their Rodney King beating, will they show their bi-racial card?

The last issue I want to discuss in this chapter is adoption, specifically transracial adoption. If White professionals admit, understand, and appreciate Black culture, they should realize family preservation is a superior choice to foster care, institutionalization, and adoption. This also applies to African American children who are taken from mainstream classrooms and placed in special education. Many social workers are quick to pull children from the home and place them in institutional and foster care rather than providing parent workshops and other resources to empower parents and children in the home.

There are approximately 50,000 African American children needing adoption. The media and some White professionals perpetuate the assumption that African American families are unwilling to adopt. The reality is many adoption agencies are not culturally sensitive to African American families; consequently White families have a much greater approval rate. Agencies that have a sincere interest in placing African American children realize their location, recruitment, screening procedures, and costs are significant. The issue is not transracial adoption, but whether or not a child's culture will be reinforced. Love from a White family is not enough in racist America, unless the child will be home schooled and work from home.

We learn racism from school curricula and the media and what more glaring example than the movie *Losing Isaiah*. Here we have a middle-class White family who wants to adopt Isiah and a low-income, single African American female addict who wants to keep the child. In the spirit of Maat and balance, the media could at least be fair and compare apples to apples. If we must consider adoption over family preservation, let's juxtapose a middle-class African American family against a middle-class White family.

An agency that understands Black culture will draw upon the rich resources of the church, which is one of our best village members. The program One Church, One Child founded by Father Clements has been very successful with over 10,000 adoptions. We have more than 75,000 churches, and while some of them are entertainment and containment, there are enough liberation churches to adopt 50,000 children who need a home. I would also suggest to some of our misinformed Black leaders and politicians, who are in favor of and voted for transracial adoption, to take heed of Minister Farrakhan's request at the Million Man March, to solicit the adoption of our children. A week later, over 5,000 families had expressed an interest in adoption.

Notes

Introduction

1) Nathan and Julia Hare, *The Endangered Black Family*. San Francisco: Black Think Tank, 1984, pp. 11-12.

Chapter Two

1) Citizens Commission on Human Rights, "Psychiatry's Betrayal," p. 13.

2) Jewelle Taylor Gibbs, ed., *Young, Black and Male in America*. Dover: Auburn House, 1988, p. 158.

   Judge Eugene Pincham, WVON Radio interview, December 4, 1990.

3) Robert Staples, *The Black Family*. Belmont: Wadsworth, 1994, p. 265.

4) William Julius Wilson, *The Truly Disadvantaged*. Chicago: University of Chicago Press, 1987, pp. 25-26.

5) ibid., p. 13.

6) Jawanza Kunjufu, *The Power, Passion and Pain of Black Love*. Chicago: African American Images, 1993, p. 24.

7) WYCA, Christian Radio Broadcast, April 10, 1992.

8) Jawanza Kunjufu, *Critical Issues in Educating African American Youth*. Chicago: African American Images, 1989, p. 17.

   Farai Chideya, *Don't Believe the Hype*. New York: Penguin, 1995, p. 75.

9) Andrew Billingsley, *Climbing Jacob's Ladder*. New York: Simon & Schuster, 1992, p. 36.

10) Black Issues in Higher Education, July 14, 1994, p. 62.

11) C. Eric Lincoln and Lawrence Mamiya, *The Black Church in the African American Experience*. Durham: Duke University Press, 1990, pp. 310, 322.

Chapter Three

1) Bette Dickerson, ed., *African American Single Mothers*. Thousand Oaks: Sage, 1995, p.55.

2) ibid., p. 87.

3) Elizabeth Achtemeir, *The Committed Marriage*. Philadelphia: Westminster, 1976, p. 22.

4) Author unknown.

5) David Blankenhorn, *Fatherless America*. New York: Harper Collins, 1995, p. 231.

   Steve Farrar, *Point Man*. Dallas: Multnomah, 1990, p. 115.

6) Four Tops, *When She Was My Girl* (cassette), "I Believe in You and Me," D. Wolfert and S. Linzer, Polygram Records, 1992.

7) Vicki Winans, *The Lady* (cassette), "The Way That You Love Me," Vicki Winans, Selah Records, 1991.

8) Renita Weems, "Sex, The Whole Matter about Intimacy and Love" (cassette), Chicago: Trinity United Church of Christ, May 20, 1995.

9) Robert Staples, *The World of Black Singles*. Westport: Greenwood Press, 1981, p. 81.

10) Jawanza Kunjufu, *The Power, Passion and Pain of Black Love*, op. cit., p. 25.

11) Weems, op. cit.

12) J. Allan Petersen, *The Myth of the Greener Grass.* Wheaton: Tyndale House, 1991, pp. 8-9.

Harley Willard Jr., *Marriage Insurance.* Old Tarpan: Revell, 1988; p. 17.

13) Robert Staples, *The Black Family.* op. cit., p. 145.

14) Achtemeir, op. cit., p. 124.

Chapter Four

1) Blankenhorn, op. cit., pp. 65, 181.

2) Farrar, op. cit., p. 115.

3) Jawanza Kunjufu, *Adam Where Are You?* Chicago: African American Images, 1994, pp. 16-17.

C. Eric Lincoln, op. cit., p. 142.

4) Blankenhorn, op. cit., p. 30.

5) ibid., p. 35.

6) ibid., p. 46.

7) Robert Staples, *The Black Family*, op. cit., p. 251.

8) Blankenhorn, op. cit., p. 42.

9) ibid., p. 129.

10) ibid., p. 134.

11) ibid., pp. 188-189.

12) ibid., p. 193.

Chapter Five

1) Oba T'Shaka, *Return to the Mother Principle of Male and Female Equality*. Volume I. Oakland: Pan Afrikan Publishers, 1995, p. 228.

2) Robert Staples, *The Black Family*, op. cit., p. 12.

3) William Julius Wilson, op. cit., p. 82.

4) M.E. Lamb and A.B. Elster, "Father-Infant Interaction," *Child Development* 13 (6), pp. 637-648.

    B.E. Robinson, "Teenage Pregnancy," American Journal of Orthopsychiatry (58 (1), pp. 46-51.

5) Frances Welsing, *Isis Papers*. Chicago: Third World Press, 1991, p. 262.

6) Bette Dickerson, op. cit., p. 152.

7) Reginald Clark, *Family Life and School Achievement*. Chicago: University of Chicago Press, 1983, p. 200.

Chapter Six

1) United States Statistical Abstract, 1994, 114th Edition, p. 475.

2) Direct Interview with ROOTS Adoption Service, College Park, Georgia, December 17, 1995.

3) Vance Packard, *Our Endangered Children*. Boston: Little, Brown, 1983, p. 71.

4) Jawanza Kunjufu, *Hip Hop vs. Maat*. Chicago: African American Images, 1993, p. 81.

5) Jawanza Kunjufu, *Developing Positive Self-Images and Discipline in Black Children*. Chicago: African American Images, 1984, pp. 73-74.

Chapter Seven

1) Tony Brown, *Black Lies, White Lies*. New York: William Morrow, 1995, pp. 12-13.

2) Deborah Prothrow-Stith, *Deadly Consequences*. New York: HarperCollins, 1991, p. 14.

3) Yosef ben-Jochannan, *African Origins of the Major Western Religions*. New York: Alkebulan Books, 1970, pp. 69-71.

4) Cornel West, *Race Matters*. Boston: Beacon Press, 1993, p. 6.

Chapter Eight

1) Frank Reid, "It's Time for New Beginnings," sermon, Men's Week, Trinity United Church of Christ, October 16, 1994, 8:00 a.m.

2) Citizen Newspaper, "From One White Slave Plantation Owner to Another," February 17, 1994, p. 20.

Chapter Nine

1) Marc Mauer, "Young Black Men and the Criminal Justice System," Sentencing Project, Washington, D.C., September, 1995.

2) Jawanza Kunjufu, *Countering the Conspiracy to Destroy Black Boys Series*. Chicago: African American Images, 1995, p. 2.

Andrew Hacker, *Two Nations*. New York: Scribners, 1992, pp. 95-96.

Chapter Ten

1) Jawanza Kunjufu, *Hip Hop vs. Maat,* op. cit., p. 113.

2) Thomas Sowell, *The Economics and Politics of Race.* New York: William Morrow, 1983, p. 155.

3) Billingsley, op. cit., p. 30.

4) ibid., p. 44.

5) Walter Malone, *From Holy Power to Holy Profit.* Chicago: African American Images, 1994, pp. 44-45, passim.

6) Jawanza Kunjufu, *Black Economics.* Chicago: African American Images, 1991, pp. 147-148.

Chapter Eleven

1) Bette Dickerson, ed., op. cit., p. 83.

2) Joyce Ladner, *Death of White Sociology.* New York: Random House, 1973, p. 439.

3) Statistical Abstract, op. cit., p. 475.

4) Earl Ofari Hutchinson, *The Mugging of Black America.* Chicago: African American Images, 1990, pp. 51-52.

5) Claud Anderson, *Black Labor, White Wealth.* Edgewood: Duncan Publishers, 1995, p. 63.

6) Statistical Abstract, op. cit., p. 48.

7) John Mbiti, *African Religions and Philosophy.* New York: Anchor Books, 1970, p. 108.

8) Thomas Kochman, *Black and White Styles in Conflict*. Chicago: University of Chicago Press, 1981, passim.

9) Brown, op. cit., p. 228.

10) Kathy Russell, Midge Wilson, Ronald Hall, *The Color Complex*. New York: Harcourt Brace Jovanovich, 1992, pp. 73-80.

NOTES

NOTES

NOTES

NOTES